CHILDREN'S AGENCY, CHILDREN'S WELFARE

A dialogical approach to child development, policy and practice

Carolus van Nijnatten

First published in Great Britain in 2013 by

The Policy Press
University of Bristol
Fourth Floor
Beacon House
Queen's Road
Bristol BS8 1QU
UK
t: +44 (0)117 331 4054
f: +44 (0)117 331 4093
tpp-info@bristol.ac.uk
www.policypress.co.uk

North American office:
The Policy Press
c/o The University of Chicago Press
1427 East 60th Street
Chicago, IL 60637, USA
t: +1 773 702 7700
f: +1 773-702-9756
e:sales@press.uchicago.edu
www.press.uchicago.edu

British Library Cataloguing in Publication Data
A catalogue record for this book is available from the British Library.

Library of Congress Cataloging-in-Publication Data
A catalog record for this book has been requested.

ISBN 978 1 44730 629 0 paperback

Cover design by The Policy Press.
Front cover: image kindly supplied by Nevit Dilmen/stockxchange.
Printed and bound in Great Britain by TJ International, Padstow.
The Policy Press uses environmentally responsible print partners.

MIX
Paper from
responsible sources
FSC® C013056

Contents

About the author

Carolus van Nijnatten was educated as a developmental psychologist at Utrecht University. For some years he worked at a child welfare agency in Amsterdam and Utrecht before returning to his former university at the end of the 1970s. In 1986 he finished his PhD thesis 'Mother Justice and her children: the development of the psycho-juridical complex in child welfare', which was also published in Germany as *Die Wahrheitsmaschine* (Forum Verlag Godesberg, 1991). From 2004 to 2009 he was Professor of Social Work at Radboud University, Nijmegen. Currently, he is Professor of Social Studies in Child Welfare at Utrecht University.

Several of his books have been published in Dutch about psychodynamic development, children's rights, case management in child welfare, authority and development, and children of detained parents. The latter was the subject of the book *Detention and development: Perspectives of children of prisoners* (Forum Verlag Godesberg, 1998). Articles by Carolus van Nijnatten have been published in *American Journal of Orthopsychiatry*, *British Journal of Social Work*, *Journal of Social Work Practice* and *Research on Language and Social Interaction*, among others. He is a member of the DANASWAC network of researchers in discourses and narratives in social work and counselling.

Carolus is the foster father of two grown-up children and lives with his partner.

Introduction

A child's need for stories is as fundamental as his need for food.
Paul Auster

Child welfare is about agency, or rather about children and families lacking adequate agency. Child welfare gets involved when children and families manifestly have serious trouble in organising their lives. As a child born of an already widowed mother who was taken into hospital on several occasions throughout my childhood, I was always aware of how vulnerable children are and how easily they can find themselves at risk. Since childhood, I have been fascinated by the vulnerability of children. When I first became a student of developmental psychology, I was already sure that my main field of study would be child welfare. I have since been involved in child welfare in various ways – as a reformer of the child welfare establishment in the 1970s, as a researcher in the field of child welfare discourse and communication, as a voluntary family guardian, and for almost 25 years as a member of the board of a child welfare agency. However, the most intense experience has been as the foster father of two children. It was from them that I learned what any parent may learn from, and tries to teach, their children: how to live one's life. For them, it was a long and difficult path to adulthood, but they demonstrated that their will to survive was stronger than the horrors they had had to endure. They also showed how hard it is to survive and to overcome the very child welfare bureaucracy that is trying to help them. Together we endured the idiocies of the system; we saw decent, hard-working social workers suffer 'burn-out' and we were astonished by the unshakeable, reigning belief in formal procedures. The best help we received was when child welfare workers did not follow the official tramlines and when we were allowed to tell our own stories.

Child welfare gets involved when parents and children are seriously at risk of losing all agency, when their behaviour signals that they lack the power to keep their lives on an even keel. For whatever reason, these people have been unable to develop the psychological means necessary to structure their lives in a complex society. Child welfare families are characterised by an accumulation of problems associated with health, work, child rearing, housing and relationships. It is an accumulation of risk factors rather than individual determinants that leads to behavioural problems.

Since the end of the 19th century, legal changes have made it possible in most western countries for the state to intervene coercively in family situations. The number of families confronted with such coercive intervention changes over time. In the Netherlands, between 1960 and 1980, there was a steady decrease in the number of child welfare interventions, but ever since, there have been a growing number of families with mandated care. Are these figures proof of declining agency among children and families or do they indicate a more repressive child welfare discourse in which the agency of children and families is questioned more than previously?

However, child welfare is also about professional agency. Over recent decades, in the Netherlands and in other European countries, professional agency has come under pressure, and has found itself under the spotlight of serious criticism. In the Netherlands, a series of fatal family dramas raised doubts about the functioning of public services. But what was remarkable about most of these tragic cases was that they provoked a general dissatisfaction with child welfare rather than condemnation of the parents or a debate on the growing difficulties that families have to face in modern, complex society. Today, little seems to be left of the professional status that social work used to enjoy in the decades following the Second World War. The profession is under fire, criticised both for its poor theoretical underpinning and for its lack of professional discipline, while behind these developments lies a decline of professional agency in a child welfare system that has increasingly become dominated by the discourse of management.

Children's and parents' agency and child welfare agency are interrelated. When civil agency becomes dysfunctional, professional agency becomes available; inadequate family agency can wind up with the intervention of a child welfare agency. Both family agency and professional agency are of an organisational nature, which enables human beings to structure their life and that of others. Agency is a complex matter, a human attribute displayed in individual development, in human interaction and social structure. In this book, the dynamics of child (development), welfare and agency will be analysed in the various different contexts in which they appear. For child development, this is the context of parenting and family life; for professional child welfare, it is the intermediate position between families at risk, professional affiliation and child welfare management; and for child welfare agencies, it is the context of political rule, citizens and institutional agencies.

A characteristic shared by both family agency and professional agency is the defensive reaction evoked whenever their quality is subjected to scrutiny. Child welfare workers know from experience that clients are on the defensive as soon as their parental capabilities and responsibilities are questioned. All too often, parents react by showering the child welfare worker with proof of their parental competence. They harden their positions and react suspiciously to any suggestions for improving the situation. One of child welfare workers' most important tasks is to encourage an exchange of information and meanings, but this defensive parental reaction can get in the way of an open dialogue with professional helpers.

One sees a similar defensive reaction on the part of child welfare workers when their own professional capabilities are raised as a subject for discussion. Mostly, they react by producing evidence of the high standard of their work, their satisfactory 'productivity' and the quality of the 'product'. 'Evidence-based child welfare' has become a slogan standing for reliability, effectiveness and professionalism. It goes without saying that rigorous evaluation of intervention programmes is a welcome support for child welfare, but the term 'evidence-based' is often used as a synonym for randomised controlled designs. The dominance of this type of evidence downgrades other kinds of research and certainly excludes professional experience as a relevant source of knowledge. In child welfare, randomised control is practically very hard to achieve. More significantly, it can only produce insight into general regularities rather than an understanding of the individual client who needs help. The dominance of this evidence-based approach, because it is concerned with determining standards rather than supporting an open dialogue with clients and colleagues about the need for change and how to achieve it, may also in the long run be counterproductive. A major task of child welfare managers is to try to organise a meaningful exchange of information and meanings between professionals. 'Evidence-based' is not the professionals' way of advancing or evaluating their own work; it is rather the way policy and client organisations demand that child welfare workers demonstrate the relevance of their work. This has put child welfare workers on the defensive.

This book is in the first instance addressed to those professionals in child welfare who think their agency is under threat, and who are convinced of the relevance of their work without it being demonstrable by means of randomised clinical trials. I hope to provide them with different modes of justification. Under pressure from modern management styles, one often hears child welfare workers nowadays say they have lost all inspiration and complain that their profession is close to losing its heart. Others suffer burn-out as they persist in a fruitless search for a balance between the demands of clients and the demands of managers, only to conclude that they cannot meet incompatible sets of expectations. There is a widespread loss of the professional self-esteem that used to enable them to accept the imperfect nature of child welfare work. With this book, I hope to give new inspiration to these professionals. To make my argument more concrete, I will introduce Jennifer. She looks much like a child welfare client I got to know. Although her story is fictitious because it involves experiences of other child welfare clients, the image that is presented of her is realistic enough.

Child welfare is a complex of relationships, institutions and agencies that needs a psycho-societal approach. It is a multifaceted institution that engages with individual development, human interaction, professional and policy interests and changing societal contexts. These different dimensions of human experience – and the ways in which they intersect – need to be studied in relation to each other. In that sense, one also hopes through this book to contribute to the development of a social scientific perspective on the relationship between individual and society mediated by professional institutions.

My main contribution will be to rehabilitate dialogue as a major instrument of organisation, at the individual, relational and institutional level. Talking was once at the heart of the social work profession. Now it has hardly a serious place in the protocols of standardisation; it cannot satisfy the demands of managers and clients for proof of quality in quantitative, measurable terms. The rehabilitation of dialogue means recognising the clinical nature of child welfare. I hope to make clear that the quality of child welfare problems lies in the realm of narrative and is dialogical.

Of course, there are also material problems, such as poverty, marginalisation and barriers to accessing facilities – all these contribute to the difficulties of child welfare families. But these difficulties only become child welfare problems at the point where they engender family turmoil, parental disorder or serious developmental problems for the child. In my own view, the response of child welfare ought to be more than plugging gaps and making up deficits; child welfare should also be concerned with parents' and children's narrative understanding of their experience and their situation in order to help them regain autonomy. The profession of child welfare is a dialogical profession. But this is not to say that scientific knowledge and professional expertise have no place; far from it. The systematic evaluation of welfare programmes is necessarily the foundation for a professional approach. Yet the child welfare professional is primarily engaged in a clinical activity of dialogical exchange with families. One can only look for the client's agency and autonomy by honouring a serious exchange of ideas and analyses and by acknowledging clients' narrative accounts of their lives. Child welfare may profit from a narrative and dialogical analysis of its work.

It is not surprising, then, that the line of thought in this book has been based on theories that pay special attention to language and dialogue. To elucidate the dialogical nature of personhood in child development, I shall rely on Lacan's linguistic interpretation of psychoanalytical theory. Contrary to what many academics and professionals may think, this theory is close to everyday experience. In her important clinical work, the Lacanian scholar Françoise Dolto (1988a) gives a detailed and pragmatic insight into the psychodynamics of child development. In her book *Tout est langage* (Everything is language), she emphasises the significance of the 'true' word. Children need words to give coherent organisation to their lives. When the relevant terms of reference are withheld, they will lack the tools needed both to understand what is happening to them and to gain a perspective on adverse experience through reflection and conversation. Words are crucial instruments for creating distance, both from self and from others, the space that allows for self-regulation and growth. The effect of traumatic experience is to disrupt and disorder this process of distancing and organising through wording. This goes not only for children and their parents but also for child welfare workers and the managers of child welfare agencies. Despite all the concentration on institutional procedures, legal rules and the efficiency of operations, words are the most relevant instruments for structuring professional practice. This is why dialogue and agency go together, not just at the level of child welfare clients but also at the level of child welfare agents.

This book could not have been produced in isolation, but only in and through dialogue with others. It would be impossible to thank all those who, through their conversation, have given me encouragement and inspiration. However, I am particularly grateful to Lynn Froggett and Nigel Parton for their commentary on an earlier version of this book, and to Murray Pearson who not only made decent English of the text but also helped to focus my arguments.

ONE

Child, welfare, agency

A new word is like a fresh seed sewn on the ground of the discussion.
Ludwig Wittgenstein

Jennifer

Jennifer is a 16-year-old girl who, since the age of two, has lived in children's homes and foster families. She has little agency and has problems maintaining relationships with other people. Whenever they come close, she pulls away. Although she was convinced that her last foster parents would always look after her, she felt she could not carry on living with the family, as she could not deal with its open character based on improvisation and mutual trust. After many rows she left home and is now trying to live on her own.

Jennifer has a history of neglect and abuse. As a baby, she lived with her parents and two elder sisters, but when it became obvious that the parents were incapable of looking after their children adequately, all three were placed in a foster family. The child welfare reports testify that she was twice taken to the hospital suffering from dehydration and that she was probably the victim of sexual abuse. Before Jennifer could even talk, her mother had threatened to throw her from the balcony if she 'did not stop trumpeting', after which Jennifer became more introverted and did not make a sound for weeks.

Throughout her young life, Jennifer was shuttled between family and agency. As soon as the relationship with her caretakers became intimate, she would find her situation unbearable and create distance for herself, often by breaking off all ties with them. It was as though she were jumping from one ice floe to another in order to survive. She learned to appraise intimacy as dangerous, and to flee to the next relationship whenever she felt she was getting too close to someone. Nonetheless, she managed to complete her schooling and started a training course to become a receptionist in an animal clinic. "Animals don't talk back", she says. For the greater part of her life, Jennifer has depended on the agency of child welfare. Apart from her last foster parents, child welfare professionals no longer play any role in her life. Although Jennifer has had mentors, personal coaches and tutors, their assistance was always provisional, at most a scaffold that might eventually enable her to construct her own life and do without their help.

Jennifer spent her infancy in a non-dialogical environment. She was silenced by her mother and this badly affected her possibilities of communication. What she learned from her mother's threats was that speaking up for oneself is dangerous. The fragility of her personal agency is due to a lack of fundamental trust in herself and in significant others, to the extent that she is scarcely able to structure her life by realising a sense of continuity. She seems to lack any internal locus of control and depends on external structures to get things straight. Time and again, she has to create an environment of security and continuity by means of formal procedures, appointments and exact phrasings. For her, words are not for expressing hope or recalling loving memories, or imagining a better future. Jennifer feels at ease when people stick precisely to their words and tries to assess her life as narrowly as possible using predetermined models of life in order to forestall any surprises. Although her style is adapted to the formal approach of child welfare bureaucracy, it is absolutely not appropriate for starting and maintaining relations in her everyday life. She takes life too literally and is incapable of irony or otherwise looking 'awry' (Žižek, 1991).

The organisation of continuity in the lives of such children as Jennifer is the very raison d'être of child welfare agencies. Ellen is one of the more than one hundred child welfare workers who have been professionally involved with Jennifer. Ellen is Jennifer's mentor during her current stay in sheltered lodgings. Ellen is 22 years old and finished secondary vocational training in welfare. This is her first job and she thinks it is exciting work; she 'loves children'. Yet she experiences her work as extremely taxing and stressful. Her own shyness and low self-esteem do not help her in her frequent conflicts with the children she deals with. She is, however, on good terms with Jennifer.

Recently, Jennifer indicated that she wanted to read her files and learn something of what happened with her parents. Jennifer has asked Ellen to accompany her when she goes to read the reports. The professional staff does not want Ellen to go with Jennifer because this role is reserved for behavioural experts. Ellen is in fact relieved; she is reluctant to escort her pupil, being afraid that the girl might lose control and ask her questions that are beyond her scope to answer.

Every six months, there is an evaluation meeting between Jennifer's guardian, the staff psychologist and Ellen. Jennifer is also invited, as are her parents, but neither they nor she attend the meetings. Each of those invited has to complete a Goal Attainment Scale and assign a score on the key issues of the care plan. Ellen confers with Jennifer about these and they fill in the same scores. Ellen does not like this kind of evaluation because she feels she cannot communicate her real assessment of her pupil's progress, she can only submit figures. Moreover, she only gives positive scores because she does not want to disappoint Jennifer. At heart, Ellen is very much concerned about Jennifer's future; she is even a little bit afraid of her. She thinks the evaluations are worthless because the only ones who really know Jennifer are not even involved in the evaluation procedure; the arrangements are made by the guardian and the psychologist, neither of whom have ever seen the girl more than once.

Ellen works in a non-dialogical environment in which she is barely able to express her observations and concerns about Jennifer in her own words. Her voice is only heard through formal channels and she does not participate in any dialogue about Jennifer's future.

Agency

Children (and adults) who have been unable to develop a minimal level of individual agency need institutional agency in order to survive. The term 'individual agency' refers to the power of individuals to manage their lives, to maintain their authenticity and autonomously make a living. 'Agency' also refers to sociocultural mediation: people can get things done through the efforts of intermediaries (Ahearn, 2001). Child welfare workers have an important intermediary function. 'Agency' is a term also used in connection with public organisations or institutions. If a family's, parent's or child's agency is at risk, professional agency is needed to make up this deficit. In this study, child, welfare and professional agency will be analysed at these three levels of individual development, interaction and social structure.

Agents are able to take an active position in life and exert an influence on the course of events. They are more motivated to take on challenges when they consider themselves as agents of their actions (Larson, 2006). That does not mean, of course, that people have total control of their life, but rather that they are intentional and purposive beings. Complete autonomy is an illusion both for children and adults, and the pursuit of complete independence is a source of major disappointment, for sooner or later a person discovers that it is unattainable. At best, most children come to realise for themselves a significant place among all the vicissitudes of an imperfect reality. In the 'good enough case', they are disillusioned gradually, meaning that they are given the chance to replace step by step the illusion of complete control with a more modest attitude to life. This becomes more likely in a dialogical context in which the child is treated as a responsible subject who actively wants to live a meaningful life within societal bounds. I take words to be the vehicles of emotions and the basic tools needed to organise one's life in ever-changing circumstances.

The idea of autonomy is closely related to that of agency and both terms have different connotations in different cultural contexts. In western cultures, agency is an individualised concept, whereas in more traditional societies greater emphasis is placed on collective agencies, but any culture has standards that differentiate normal and pathological agency.

Agency is analysed as a capacity that is developed in a dialogical context. As Garfinkel (1967) argues, human agents, as ideal-typical actors, do not embody social patterns in a docile way, but rather operate in different ways in various here-and-now contexts. Agency belongs to individuals, social powers and institutions. In the context with which this book is concerned, the concept of individual agency is related to professional agency in child welfare agencies and personalisation policies. 'Professional agency' refers again to an organisation's capacity to arrange and to manage. Just like children and parents, child welfare workers and their agencies may be held responsible for their performances. The starting point of this book is that the same kinds of process play a role in developing agency in children, in repairing agency in troubled parents, and in developing professional agency in child welfare and the agency of agencies. Dialogue is the key word to understanding the processes that enable agency to mature.

So, agency is of social origin. Becoming independent is a gradual transition from other-regulation to self-regulation. Vygotsky's idea was that in lived speech and interaction with others, children learn how to organise their life. Wertsch (2008) explains that the mechanisms that make the transition from other- to self-regulation possible is the result of the child's attempts to establish coherence between her own action and the adult's speech. In this process, the child adjusts her definition of the situation consistent with her behaviour rather than carry out a task because she shares the adult's definition of the situation (Wertsch, 1979, p 78).

Making sense

There is no inherent sense in reality itself. Camus (1955) symbolises the human condition with Sisyphus, who was condemned by the Gods to ceaselessly rolling a rock to the top of a mountain, whence the stone would fall back of its own weight, indicating the absurd enterprise of life. Humanity can be seen as one huge effort to avoid meaninglessness (Žižek and Daly, 2004). Spoken and written words enable people to construct a sense of continuity. What makes a people a society is speaking more or less the same language, whose development depends on the contributions of its members, producing a common sense. Physical, biological and historical phenomena only become part of the human world at the moment individuals reflect on them by means of language (compare Bruner, 1990). Words humanise the senseless world of objects and make that world comprehensible (Dolto, 1984), and yet people never fully succeed in obliterating the void beneath them. In the very attempt to approach reality with signifiers, language creates distance and reality slips away. Our conception of the world can never be complete.

The words that individuals choose to describe and understand 'their' world stem from a cultural, trans-individual vocabulary. Individual wordings are always of social origin. By using this vocabulary and by speaking, individuals add to the development of language and the advance of culture. As Berger and Luckman (1971) said, man's self-production is always a social enterprise, and social order an ongoing production of human origin. Processes of making sense are both individual and social. People organise their lives by giving meaning to life events and by presenting themselves, predominantly through narratives (Holstein and Gubrium, 2000). In their narratives, they summarise happenings and place them in a certain order, they position these events in time and space, and give meaning to them. Mostly, they tell the outcome of the developments and how this influences their actual position (Labov, 1972). The consciousness of being one and the same person over time is the outcome of these presentations. In speaking, people emphasise their subjectivity and reinforce their relationship with the people around them whose language they speak. In their stories, people are revealing the truth, not in an effort to approach an objective reproduction as it actually was, but rather the truth of their experience. That is why not only narratives are forms of interpretation but also need interpretation to understand (Riessman, 1993).

People can only live their lives together if they can make themselves understood. Using culturally shared concepts to describe their identity, they become aware of who they are. Societal development depends on its members' contributions, making sense not only of their individual lives but also of their relationships with others, producing common sense. This shared ground is the foundation of social institutions such as schools, the law and welfare. Communication as the exchange of meaning between people plays a key role in complex societies in which millions of people share ideas, desires and plans. People share experience by exchanging signs; in their voices their different perspectives may be heard (Bakhtin, 1986). Words carry experience from one person to another. This is never a perfect transference, as a good dialogue actually profits from the active recognitions and awareness of constraints and misunderstanding (Stiles, 1999).

Each baby is a fresh kernel in a world full of meanings. The extraordinary potential of the newborn infant may be developed further in life, but she or he also has to fit into the straightjacket of cultural limitations and it is a long, hard journey for this tiny biological creature to become a member of a culture. In a very short time, the infant has to become familiar with a long cultural history and in order to become a member of society the child has to restrict its own desires.

The well-being of children is dependent on a complex of biological, developmental and social factors. How the child's genetic potential will unfold is a matter of nurture. At the start of her life, the child does not possess an internal psychic instrument to direct her life; she has little agency and is dependent on the help of its caregivers to create continuity. In other words, the development of individual agency is an interaction between personal traits and social conditions. Neither social structure nor individuality is primary; rather, both are mutually dependent. Individual agency is an individual attribute that is acquired socially. Developing their agency, children gain more individual power to structure their lives and to take important decisions.

This book considers developmental processes in the very early stages of life, in the context of parental care, their relevance the disturbances and inadequacies in the lives of children, in the context of broken homes, and to the help extended by child welfare to these children. The aim is to explore child, welfare and agency at the levels of individual development, family (dis)continuity, child welfare and organisation. Identity and agency appear at the levels of personality, interaction and social structure (Coté and Levine, 2002) – interaction between society and individual. Relational patterns and social norms are reproduced and actualised in interactions between people, and in these interactions individual identities are constructed. The three levels are interdependent but none can be reduced to another.

The approach fits in with recent developments in developmental psychology in which children's agency is described as an embodied, dynamic and reflective self, participating in different contexts and social interactions with other beings and things (Hermans, 1996; Martin, 2006; Valsiner, 2006; Chandler and Proulx, 2008; Martin et al, 2008).

Jennifer was raised by parents who had little capacity to organise their daughter's life; they were too much involved with themselves and the child had little chance to develop agency. The words spoken by the parents were hardly ever aimed at Jennifer and did not help her to get her life organised; she had poor experience in presenting herself in a confidential environment. When she was admitted to child welfare, the professionals involved were not able to repair the damage done, partly because child welfare policy is disciplinary rather than dialogical.

Continuity

Human agency is closely related to the ability to construct psychological continuity. People look for ways to understand themselves as one and the same person over time and in different locations. Their appearance, sense of well-being and surroundings may change, but they describe their various ways of being as instances of one and the same person. These descriptions may change over time, but always have enough connection with former descriptions to maintain a recognisable link between past and future. Continuity is an inner temporal awareness that helps people to contain the past and anticipate the future; the past does not sink into nothing but remains significantly present in the memory. People who do not understand that their past contributes to their personality or are unaware that their actual conduct qualifies their future personhood cannot be held fully responsible for any deviant conduct (Harré, 1979).

There is no essential source of temporal awareness, but rather a developing psychic constellation, an 'I' that grows by identifications in meaningful communication with others. This psychic entity protects the subject against internal or external interruptions (Frosh et al, 2003). In order to be able to live as one and the same person, people need to see and acknowledge similarities in ways of being in the various periods of their life and retrospectively to see these as belonging to their own person (Chandler et al, 2003). The self is a constantly actualised narrative of who somebody is in relation to others. Individuals do not simply play the main role in their biography, they are also the ones who tell the story and actively construct it (Gergen and Gergen, 1983). Moreover, whether in externally or internally directed speech, these narratives are always expressed before a(n internalised) audience. New narrative elements appear (I am married; I hope to start a course in psychology; my father died) and old ones disappear. New narratives of the self may be necessary adaptations to a changed context, but continuity is ensured if they are related to the former narratives. If one cannot recover old elements in the new stories, it becomes impossible to represent a meaningful self along these new lines. In this case, a therapist may help to co-construct and individual's experiences in new meanings.

Continuity is thus the result of dialogical processes in which (self) images are produced and reproduced. People create stability where originally there was instability. They create the illusion of living a stable life in the present by constructing an identity (Valsiner, 2006). The construction of continuity is not solely a matter of language per se; it also depends on the exchange of meaningful words in a human dialogue (Hermans and van Kempen, 1993), in a personalised relationship. With increasing age, people acquire better tools with which to guarantee the stability of their identity, the narrative of their lives. The capacity to reflect on this narrative is particularly important as a means to preserve the coherence of one's life. The personality is layered, the philosopher and psychologist William James proposed, and beside the 'I' there is 'me', a reflective self. This is the foundation of a triangulation and enables the person to construct continuity and coherence in daily experiences. Pre-adolescent children often deny that it is possible to both change and to remain the same person; they can only entertain the idea of remaining the same by denying change or by minimising the influence of such changes (Chandler, 2000). Most adolescents have learned to imagine the self in abstract terms and see changes as partial or trivial shifts in relation to a constant self. They place changes in a continuing line that relates past, present and future. Chandler and Ball (1990) found that adolescents who are uncertain about their identity and who think that suicide is still the only option have a very poor sense of personal continuity.

Our case study Jennifer lacks a solid awareness of continuity, being unable to trust herself as someone capable of relying on in different situations. She is nervous of any new situation and prefers to make very clear arrangements in order to avoid surprises. Scarcely hearing her own voice, she has developed hardly any interactive agency. After a few months, her mentor Ellen learned how to deal with this and prepared Jennifer for future steps to take. Her foster father now uses his mobile phone to get in touch with her and to announce his visits. In a few months, Jennifer will move out of her sheltered lodgings and will have to deal with people who are unaware of her psychological and interactive deficiencies. How will she deal with the unpredicted nature of everyday life?

Dialogue

Human development begins in dialogue, children learning to organise their world through interaction with others. Children need a responsive environment in order to develop agency at different levels. Only then do they learn to become active participants in everyday life. Parenting demands both acknowledgment and restriction of the child. Child rearing is a social undertaking that depends on suitable dialogical conditions in family proximity and in the wider society. People emphasise their individuality by speaking for themselves, but at the same time bind themselves to the order of the language and the symbols they use in speech. The use of symbols enables people to create distance from reality and from bystanders, and to take a position vis-à-vis each other. They can see the past *as* past and project themselves into the future.

A person's experience of reality has both cognitive and affective components that mutually act on each other. On the one hand, what a person feels about another person or situation is in part determined by prior (assumed) knowledge of that person or situation. On the other hand, people cannot know the world in an objective way because the world always primarily *affects* us in one way or another (Mooij, 2010). People do not look at something or somebody, but they aim for something and long for someone. *How* we think cannot be divorced from *what* we think.

To become a member of a society, one has to speak the language of the culture. Language is not just an instrument for describing reality; it is something we use to help us understand reality, to grasp it and to construct new meanings from what we see and believe to be 'out there' beyond ourselves. With words, people give meaning to themselves, their lives and their relationships. As soon as people talk with each other, they create and recreate a common condition. It is the exchange of meanings rather than language per se that counts. For people to understand each other and to achieve intersubjectivity, they have to transcend their personal worlds. This demands mutual presentation, an acceptance of roles (Rommetveit, 1984) and a framework. Identity, rather than having an immutable core, is a social representation that constantly changes as a result of negotiations in exchanges with other people (Grossen and Salazar Orvig, 1998). In dialogues, feelings are verbalised and identities presented to other people. The outcomes are negotiable rather than predetermined; different personal and general views are attuned in an effort to reach a common understanding about what the world is like. The rules of society that constrain and direct people in their speech and activities form the framework that makes it possible for people to understand each other. People show their acceptance of societal rules by adhering to them and as such are aware of the consequences of their behaviour (Duintjer, 1977). Each speaking person is a continuation of societal life from a unique position in time and space. In this way, the individual confirms the survival and embodiment of society.

Children become members of society when they begin to use its language and symbols. Through speech, they become subject to societal rules and regulations and acknowledge other people's individual positions. They talk a common language rather than a private one, one that had its existence before they were born and will remain unaffected by their death. Any self-expression in language therefore has an aspect of alienation, but at the same time, it is an acknowledgement of social ties. In their use of a common language, people transcend their individual situation and share an understanding – an understanding that is, however, provisional rather than fixed, an ongoing process of generating and exchanging new meanings. In different contexts, the individual takes other positions that may be the opposite of a previous position or mutually reinforcing. Changing meta-positions rather than one central overarching position help the individual to organise the relationship between these various positions (Gergen and Gergen, 1983; Sampson, 1985; Hermans and van Kempen, 1993).

Jennifer grew up in a non-dialogical environment; her mother simply told her to shut up. She was made speechless. Although she was taught to speak in her childhood, she did not learn to express her experiences or emotions in words. It was as if she only felt comfortable if words were spoken with univocal meaning and exclusive intent. In the absence of confidence in herself, Jennifer looked for fixed arrangements and clear-cut statements.

Jennifer did not feel at ease in the foster family in which she was received because her foster parents talked a different language, full of ambiguity and improvisation. She felt happier without intimacy in the institutional context of child welfare, in frequently changing relationships with peers and staff and with a well-structured environment. Her own feelings remained trapped in her inner world, unexpressed.

The rise of provisional truths

What we know of the inner world of children and their parents is what we learn by listening to them. We shall hardly understand them if we look at them from the outside and seek objective measures. We can only try to recognise what is happening if we approach them as sensible subjects making meaning of their lives. The same goes for the performances of child welfare agents. We shall only learn about child welfare work if we acknowledge professionals as human agents who try to do a significant job in helping their clients.

The premise of this book is the idea that one can learn a great deal about child welfare families and about child welfare interventions if one looks for the agency of children, parents, professionals and organisations. Their statements, expressions and accounts are the starting point for the analyses presented in this book, which takes a constructivist and dialogical approach to look for parallels between child development, parenting and professional child welfare. Despite this theoretical approach, both texts and conversations form the empirical basis of the theories and analyses, being neither the exclusive source of meaning nor the outcome of (macro-social) factors (Hall et al, 2006).

I start from the constructivist idea that there is no split between human reality and the observation of it. The world is not waiting out there to be discovered, but only appears at the moment of observation and interpretation. Discourse is a mode of action and representation at the same time (Fairclough, 1991). The world is rapidly changing with new truths and paradigms. Society is no longer dominated by clearly defined categories of social class, sex and age, and normative dichotomies of good and bad, black and white, and sick and healthy (Foucault, 1982). These categorisations have not only been contested and lost their previous authority; rather, the whole mechanism of social control by categorisation would seem to be under review and individuals rather than groups are these days at the centre of the guidelines of social policy. People follow their own course and are not determined by the grand narratives. Change and multiformity have become positive values (Lyotard, 1984) and people are judged on their acquired rather than on their traditional roles. The existent is put into perspective by the understanding that everything might have been different; the world is contingent and our understanding is ambivalent. There is no underlying, objective truth to be sought in everyday human affairs. 'Truth' is unmasked as the product of our activities and observations.

A constructive approach may lead to multiformity and qualification, but there is also the danger that it can easily lead to relativism and the pessimistic idea that there is nothing beyond a fragmented world, while local and temporary descriptions offer no coherent account by which one can structure everyday life. Constructivist descriptions are local and provisional, but within this context there is no reason why they should not be coherent and useful. Fay (1996) proposes a critical intersubjectivity that allows for the description and discussion of different theories of observation of all kinds of phenomena, in an 'ongoing dialogue among rival inquirers each of whom accepts to understand the others in a manner genuinely open to the possibility that their views may have merits' (p 213). 'Reality' as we perceive it is constantly changing, but that does not mean that a provisional truth cannot be found in local configurations. Constructivism does not negate the idea of the subject, nor does it imply the futility of all hopes of realising social coherence. It is rather the acknowledgment that people start from different historical backgrounds and try to forge meaningful communities without anyone having the right to assert the priority or authority of any of the choices that are made.

This view has consequences for the way we look at development, at raising children, at the source of family problems and at how to solve them. The following chapters are concerned with continuity and discontinuity in child development and parenthood, and with the attempts by child welfare agencies to restore continuity. A constructivist and dialogical view of child welfare is allied to a critical and problematising approach with regard to the 'facts' and 'certainties' about these lives and relationships in families with problems. People construct their interpretations of reality in daily interactions, their relationship with the child welfare agent being a salient example. That is why this book pays particular attention to the dialogical character of the helping relationship. In this context, the term 'constructive' refers to the fact that there is no single, optimal way to carry out child welfare with perfect strategies and techniques, but rather that child welfare is a productive and positive process in which new narratives may help clients to restore the continuity in their lives (Parton and O'Byrne, 2000).

Parents and children often have a long history of relational disappointment, family problems and social isolation. The child's first confrontation with child welfare is the start of a period with new breaches and interventions. I start from the idea that there is no single solution for all the problems that families face, for the difficulties of child welfare agents or for the problems that child welfare agencies are confronted with in their efforts to organise family interventions in a professional manner. Neither there is one ideal interactive pattern between parents and children, between professionals and clients and among professionals themselves (compare Hall and Slembrouck, 2009). Pursuing the single, optimal strategy, intervention or communication would be a risky approach that would be more likely to create new problems than to solve them. Agency – whether of individual children, their parents or child welfare workers and their agencies – cannot be perfect. Just as children need 'good enough' parents, society needs a 'good enough' child welfare practice.

In the end, this book is itself an imperfect contribution to an imperfect child welfare practice. But acknowledging that perfection is unattainable does not relieve us from the responsibility of trying as best we can. We can do this by opening up a dialogue about child welfare and then going on to discuss its various aspects.

TWO

The development of individual agency

It's only children, in fact, only infants who feel a wish and its fulfilment as one; perhaps this is what gives tyrants their childish air. *Ian McEwan*

This chapter deals with the process of entering into human society, which all children undergo. It is difficult for any child to learn that in changing circumstances she and the people around remain constant. Spatial and temporal experience only begins after separation from the womb in which the infant was one with her mother, protected from the tensions of intensifying and decreasing needs. Human beings are forever being shuttled between experiences of fusion with the other and coming out on their own.

The problems young children have with constructing continuity show early on, in functions such as their bowel movements. It is by no means unusual for infants to panic when they see their stool in the pot. Noticing that something has fallen from their body, they – quite logically – conclude that their self has been diminished. They have yet to learn that when we eat, although we still view our bodies as more or less unchanged, the bodily situation actually changes. If someone disappears from the infant's life, she may assume that part of herself has disappeared and may panic in the same way. The developmental task of the infant is to learn that she remains the same person despite that loss or absence. Young children panic easily because they perceive instances of change as absolute changes and are unable to use symbols to distance themselves from such events. They are dependent on the situation: when the environment changes, the child changes. Psychological continuity is the development of the notion of remaining one and the same self, in spite of changes.

The child has an image of her physical appearance that enables her to conceive of herself. In order to internalise a stable picture of herself as someone who remains the same person despite physical and environmental changes, the child has to imaginatively override a reality that is actually changing all the time. From the moment that the infant takes a position towards her body and the surrounding world, she becomes capable of maintaining psychological continuity. She has then understood that the taking and excreting of fluids, the growth and decline of physical capabilities, meeting and missing people all involve changes but that these do not lead to a change of person. The infant ignores the 'logical conclusion' that the 'I' is continually appearing and disappearing or reappearing in qualitatively different form. The child, as it were, 'feigns' a psychological unity, whereas in fact the conditions both in and around the body are permanently changing. Taking the 'I' as a reality is a *necessary* misrepresentation (Lacan, 1949).

Françoise Dolto (1998) gives a striking example of a boy of four, who, having recently moved into a new house with his parents, thought that in the new house his father would also be a new father. This is the logic of an infant who thinks that his father will change if the house changes, who is not yet able to entertain the idea that in spite of change, certain persons and things remain unchanged. Nobody has explained to him which things will change and which will not. He identified his father with the things in the former home and thought that changing these things would also change the father. The boy did not alter his attitude towards his father; what he lost in moving to another house were the identifying markers.

During development, the *awareness* of constancy becomes a linguistic construct, the child using words to connect different situations and underline what remains unchanged among the altering conditions, for instance by using personal pronouns. The linguistic exchange of meanings enables the child to draw a line of continuity through the transformations to which he is subjected. Dialogue plays a crucial role in perceiving a world with steady distinguishing markers. Infants can only partially draw on linguistic instruments to draw such a line of continuity and progress; in early childhood in particular they must rely on their parents. In his new house, the four-year-old boy could not imagine that at six o'clock the same father would come 'home'. His parents could have prepared him for the psychological step demanded by the new situation, for instance by visiting the new house with him before the move and by mentioning who and what would move with them to the new house.

Language forms the basis of human development; it is at the core of personal and social identity. Identity may be a fiction, but it is a vital fiction for becoming a person and for making coherent past experiences, actual feelings and acts, and future projections. Human identity has a narrative character; the person structures his or her life with the help of stories and so constructs an experience of continuity. Should the child fail to build a narrative structure out of these images and symbols, she would be absorbed into the meaningless void of reality.

A very young infant does not yet use language in an active way, but is involved in linguistic interactions passively. The child is talked to and presented with an image of her person in her parents' terms. During the course of development, the child herself learns to use language to represent her identity and to structure interactions with others. A crucial step is the 'discovery' that language refers to something that is not immediately present. The child is now able to represent something that in fact is absent, opening up new horizons and marking the rise of desire (a longing for what is absent). The child's verbal constructions are related to the context in which they are told. If her stories were unconnected with physical and social reality, a discontinuity would arise; the child would then be unable to find the words needed to make the physical and social reality intelligible to herself and others.

In the course of her development, the child gains a more active role in structuring her life. In their symbolic use, stories help the child to establish her own distance, no longer totally absorbed by life. In fact, the child has a multi-voiced self, which arises as a result of the adoption during infant development of different internal and external 'positions' (Hermans and van Kempen, 1993; Bertau, 2004). Children's narratives are the outcome of dialogical negotiations between different 'positions' within the child self and between the child and other individuals. Adults who assume the responsibility of raising a child accompany the child's entrance into society. At the time of entry and at subsequent moments when the child's social situation changes radically, words are major tools in accomplishing those changes. Increasingly, the child herself will tell her story and construct and reconstruct her own and others' lives.

Certainty and continuity

At first, children learn without being able to explain the underlying principles of what they have been taught (Wittgenstein, 1969). They grow up in an environment that they accept as natural, unaware of any ideation behind this 'natural' façade (for that would imply that they were capable of conceiving anything beyond the immediate reference of this situation). They take the association between word and thing for granted; they have a 'groundless' trust in things (Duintjer, 1977). The child surrenders to the world that is presented. The parents' words represent a system of meanings and values within which the child will grow up and so become part of a self-evident framework from which, with development, the child will be able to reason and distinguish truth from untruth. This is not to say that the growing child thinks the same as its caregivers, but that she starts from a common (back)ground with the same in-built assumptions about what is 'natural'. Only much later, children come to learn different words that have different meanings and learn that the same words may have different meanings in different contexts (Wittgenstein, 1953).

Babies are aware of the emotional import of words. The words that are spoken in welcome or to comfort are signs of recognition and acceptance in the community. Hearing such words, without needing further evidence, the infant accepts that her caregivers have reserved a place for her. The question of loving or not loving one's parents does not arise with children. Even if the child were not particularly fond of her parent, this would not change the 'naturalnessness' of the relationship. From this grows the basic trust that children need in order to go out in the world. Children who never hear words of recognition and acceptance in infancy are often condemned (for the rest of their lives) to search for evidence that other people accept them. Like Jennifer, they cannot take for granted that they will be accepted.

When an infant is welcomed as a member of the family, he or she receives a name that symbolises the psychological space reserved for him or her in the family and the wider social world. Adults repeatedly point at the child's image and repeat his or her first name until, finally, the child grasps the association between the image and the words 'This is John' or 'This is Mary' and understands that John or Mary is his or her name. The child neither questions whether this is 'really' the case, nor needs convincing that he is indeed John. There is no proof, because the identification with the image is a psychological construction beyond any question of factuality. The fact is that an essential identity is lacking. There is no 'true' reflection or a 'true' image that would help the child to develop an essential self, for the self at this stage is no more than the accepted construction offered by parents. What the child does is to identify with a fiction that is presented from the outside (Lacan, 1949). In other words, the 'I' cannot to be reduced to an inner core substrate that coincides with the child's perception of her reality. The child simply has to take for granted the image that others present of it. Only then is the child able to say, 'That's me'. The first name accompanies the child from birth to death. We are probably scarcely aware of how often young children hear their first name. The child's name is related to the image of her body and her position towards other people. The child's identification with the name is necessary to develop a personal identity and to adopt the cultural programme in which she is raised as a natural background. From this background, she will learn to discriminate, select and think.

The child is ignorant not only in the way he acts but also in his desires. People around the child play a major role in the development of the *will*. The child's desires, his ambitions, strivings and longings have their foundation in the desire of the parents, which can be very strong. During the first year of life, the child has a symbiotic relation with his parents. The child distinguishes himself from the parents but cannot do without them. People around the infant help him to name himself with his first name, the name that will be an anchor for the continuity of self-consciousness. How do words contribute to this psychological development of the child? To answer this question, I will adopt the concepts of 'body schedule' and 'body image' from the theoretical account of Françoise Dolto (1984). The term *body schedule* is used to refer to the individual's physical conditions: bodily changes, motor possibilities and impossibilities. The body schedule is the intermediary between the subject and the surrounding world; it is unrelated to language and functions especially at the level of fulfilment of needs. The *body image*, on the other hand, is the individual's psychological representation of his or her body, by means of which the subject translates reality into understandable terms; it makes the body navigable. The body image does not necessarily give an accurate representation of the actual physical conditions. If, according to his body schedule, a child is capable of eating with a fork, the child is physically able to hold a fork and to pick up and bring the food to the mouth. The body image may lag behind this schedule, because in that image it is the mother who has to hold the fork and should feed the child. In a psychological sense, the child has not yet separated from the mother. For successful development, body image and body schedule need to be aligned so that the child can learn to take care of himself, to 'mother himself' (Corveleyn and Traversier, 1998). A child who still *wants* to drink from the breast (in conformity with a body image), when he no longer needs it to feed himself (according to the body schedule), develops an (erotic) desire for the mother's breast. In the request to drink from the breast, the child is expressing more than mere just thirst; he also shows that he wants a constantly available mother. At first, the mother will corroborate this attitude by approving the child's demand, calling the child the sweetest and most beautiful child in the world. The mother is everything for the child until the moment she refuses him with such words as 'You can now eat all by yourself'. When the mother utters these words of refusal, she also offers something: the word replaces her breast. Mother's words function symbolically and bring about a change of desire – from desire for erotic satisfaction to desire for an intimate communication between two subjects who love each other (Dolto, 1984). Through this dialogue the child gains another body image and learns to treat physical stimuli in a different way. In the child's future development, talk will always be connected to the mother's desire and to the longing for her and other primary caregivers. The act of affectionately restructuring the child's life – through affectionate but resolute refusal – leads to the gradual disillusionment of the child and acceptance of the presence of the real (m)other (Winnicott, 1985).

The body image is the synthesis of a child's personal emotional history and the words spoken over the course of this history and remembered by the child. One of the major tasks of those who raise the child (or in the case of therapy, the therapist) is to inform the child about his physical position, to relate his history, where he was born, who loved him and what decisions were taken. The child's body image enables him to present himself as a human being and assume a position in time and place. Only if the child is able to express what is happening in his body in words that are intelligible to others is it possible to relate to those others, to take a position as someone who wants something and who hopes that others will love him. Without the support of that image, the body schedule would be closed to communication.

In a busy street, I once overhead a mother saying to her baby daughter in a buggy, "Then Mummy puts the letter in 'Other destinations'". The infant, however, would have lacked the cognitive capacity to understand that the mother was going to post a letter and that in doing so she had the choice between posting it in the slot for local destinations and another for other destinations. Nor would the mother in all probability have had any intention of explaining this to the child. She simply meant to put the child at her ease by talking to her. Seated in the buggy, the child would have been overwhelmed by the confusion of outside stimuli – harsh light, the smell of traffic fumes, the noise of bicycle bells – all without being able to see her mother who was pushing her from behind, outside of her field of vision. The sound of the mother's voice would probably have been the only point of recognition in this entire chaotic buzz of stimuli. Her function is to create a holding environment that helps the child to integrate in the social world; this needs an attentive parent who is able to imagine himself or herself in the child's situation (van Nijnatten, 2006a).

The infant who cannot yet use words to signify the world around her is dependent on the structure created by bystanders with their recognisable faces, voices and smells. The child identifies in an imaginary way, which is to say that she adds a psychic dimension to the finiteness of the own body and begins to experience this as a unity called 'I', which enables the child to differentiate herself from others, although she observes those others as qualitatively the same as herself, rather than different. The earliest identity of the infant 'I' involves an unmediated incorporation of the proximate object as well as self, overlapping the existence of the other. The person of the other does not really matter, just as when one is in love (Barthes, 1977).

The infant finds herself in a state of total dependence, sensing unity with those who care for her. Changes in the surroundings have a direct impact on the child; words have an indicative function and do not yet refer to other moments or places. The child's idea of the world is built not on images that are pointed out and the words that accompany these images. Children take things at face value. Sound, smell and facial recognition are the most important instruments for making associations. The child is already capable of recognising smells, sounds and sights and the traces of these recollections form her first firm stepping stone. Nursing a baby, or holding her while bottle feeding, has a major psychological significance. Repetition of this experience evokes recognition and gives the child a sense of continuity. From the moment of first intense physical contact, the distance between infant and surrounding objects and people is bridged. Recognition is only possible if repeated experiences are also linked to new sensations. The parental voice, smell and face, and as well as the socially constructed rhythms and patterns of sleeping and being awake, shape routines of regularity and constancy that become integrated into the child's sense of self (Bruner, 1983).

The foundations of a complex mental apparatus are laid during the first years of life, which is necessary for organising the relationship between the individual body and the social context. The child constructs the relationship between her body and others by means of images and symbols. Both the image that helps the child to form a sense of 'I' and the symbol used to signify the (different) position to others are alien in the sense that they are neither innate nor perfect but are given through interaction with a pre-existing social and linguistic order. Lacan (1973) uses the term 'suture' to refer to the idea that an individual can never fully represent herself in and by language, that the 'I' of the language can never fully represent the self. The 'I' is not an essence but merely a representation. We have to identify with something we are not, so that nothing we ever say about ourselves is a perfect statement; there is always something left to be said.

The first sense of coherence – that is, the feeling of being an 'I' – thus stems from the images that are reflected by other people and so have a social origin. The symbols the child later uses to differentiate between others also come from the environment in which the child grows up. The child necessarily uses the cultural signs in her communication with others; the child must speak the language of the society in order to become a member of that society. Although in the case of a 'good' development, the child will accept the imaginary and symbolic 'I' as its essential self, the foundations and their imperfection remain unfamiliar. Agency is an imperfect rather than a complete psychological organisation. The modernist view of a world with completely rational and reflective human actors is no more than a fantasy (Campbell, 1996).

Humanising words

The first words the child speaks indicate present objects and persons. At this stage, there is no relationship as yet between language and internal cognitive activities (Piaget, 1968). This does not mean that the child is incapable of pre-linguistic communication with people around him. The infant is already able to differentiate between several ways of asking for attention and soon develops more ways of interaction in which exchange and reciprocity develop little by little. The child's language acquisition is not a purely cognitive process but rather a dialogical phenomenon. From the very first moment, the child plays an active role in the communication with the primary caregivers (Bruner, 1975). Infants' linguistic development is not only based on an imitation of sounds but also on parental responsiveness, for instance when the parent laughs or touches the child in reaction to his jabber (Goldstein et al, 2003).

Infants' language only refers to the direct relations between the environment and the child; what is happening outside that situation cannot yet be described. At the end of their second year, children start using language in a symbolic way, referring to persons and things not present in their immediate environment (Ginsburg and Opper, 1969). For example, when they can say of a Lego object that 'the house is not yet ready', they are demonstrating their ability to entertain a mental concept of a house yet to be built. The symbolic use of language begins at the moment that the child becomes conscious that important caregivers are temporarily absent. At first, this is a frightening experience because the child, with her limited physical and mental capacities, is still dependent on the care of others. The child may feel her existence threatened because she cannot yet imagine existence without the other person. The radical nature of this process becomes clear when children defecate in the pot for the first time, as discussed at the beginning of this book. The first sight of their own stool may put them into a total panic. The child cannot yet put this loss into perspective and is totally dependent on what the environment gives and takes. It is still a question of all or nothing. The desperation is the result of a correct observation of the actual events, even too correct an observation, because the child is still incapable of detachment. Something has fallen out of her body and the logical conclusion is that the child now has become less 'I'. The infant is overwhelmed by that experience. What will happen if more should fall out? The developmental task of the child is to acknowledge that 'I' will still be there after the change. The ritual of flushing the stool down the toilet is not just a parental habit, but also an essential act of support for the child to help her master this change.

The same happens if a parent disappears for a while. The child then also feels her existence threatened because the one who gives meaning to her life seems to have vanished. The child's task is to grasp with words that life will continue after loss. Freud showed in his famous Fort-Da observation how a child literally manipulates presence and absence by using a play object. The child throws away an object that is tied to a string and, dumbfounded, calls out 'Fort' (gone), symbolising the parent's departure. She then retrieves the object, gaily calling out 'Da' (here), putting the parent's return into words. 'Fort' and 'Da' were obviously the words used by the parent when they told the child they would be 'Fort' for a moment but would soon be 'Da' again. The parent has gone, but the words remain (Mannoni, 1967) and assume their place in the child's structure of desire, because they refer to the object of desire, the parent. The function of words at these moments of transfer is crucial. By using language in a symbolic way, the child can represent the other, in spite of his or her absence. The departure is replaced by a sign that refers to what was lost. The child can only gain autonomy if she is able to put these losses into words. If a child fails to put into words what becomes lost, there are no words to fill the emptiness and the child will suffer loss of sense. Compulsory repetition may be the pathological reaction in which unconscious relational patterns are repeated. If words do not come, actions will appear in an effort to forget (Nicolaï, 2003) or to fill the gap.

With children, open communication is a necessary precondition for a child's undisturbed development. It is therefore important that, right from the beginning, parents talk with their children. Young children may not understand the precise cognitive meaning of what is told to them, but they do grasp its emotional charge (van Nijnatten, 2006a). When their parents have trouble in verbalising their feelings; they understand that these are difficult or bad feelings that are better not discussed. They may even assume that they are the cause of these feelings. If, on the contrary, the parent says, "Sweetheart, I am in pain, but that has nothing to do with you", the child shows immediate relief (Dolto 1988b). An open dialogue in which the caregivers meet the child as a dialogical parent from whom no secrets are withheld creates good conditions for trust and continuity. If the infant cries, and the caregiver does not understand why, she or he can say, "I don't know why you are crying, but do you want to tell me anything?" This may not stop the suffering, but the words humanise the child's feelings. The words that accompany the parent's actions, (re)construct the relationship between the child's body schedule and body image. "I am going to run your bath; I am going to make your bottle"; the word remains with the child as the parent leaves.

In order to help the child to open up to the world, it is necessary to talk to the child and to bring feelings into words. These are not always sweet words, because an angry parent expresses his or her anger where a mild parent would use friendly words, but the child is told what the parent is doing, thinking or feeling (Dolto, 1994). That does not mean that anything that enters a parent's mind should be expressed, but rather that there should be a feeling of sincerity and openness about what matters to the child. If parents are unable sincerely to position their child and to disguise their own uncertainties and anxieties, this can engender an insecure relationship between the child's body image and body schedule. Keeping secrets therefore, for instance, about past neglect, intended divorce or the child's biological parentage, will ultimately harm the child rather than protect her. The child will later experience the effects of the neglect, the parental separation or the lack of information about her birth origins. Withholding relevant information will only confuse the child, teaching her there are things that are better not talked about.

Development by limitation

The child who takes up a symbolic position will recognise (sexual) difference; the acceptance of being different from others is one of the basic conditions of individuality. It is a gradual process of the separation of self and other, leading to self-cohesion. (Kohut, 1978). The achievement of an individual position is only possible when the child acknowledges the *subjectivity* of her position, and can subordinate herself to the language by means of which she articulates herself. Although imperfect, this subjective position will take a leading role in the organisation of the child's life. Most developmental and psychological theories assume such meta-position (Hermans, 2004) or 'over-arching structure in the human mind' (Neimeyer and Buchanan-Arvay, 2004). Vygotsky (Wertsch, 1985) presupposes the capacity for reflection in a generalised way. Lacan (1958) describes the subjective position as the possibility of reflecting within a triangular structure, enabling the person to detach him or herself from the immediate environment. A meta-position mediates between the person and the environment, and prevents the subject becoming the plaything of others, unable to govern his or her own life. An important function for those who raise a child is to help the child to avoid the danger of getting lost in an unpredictable and confusing struggle between 'I' positions, essentially by providing an external overarching structure, helping the child to build an internal one herself.

The limitation of desire plays an important role in the child's development. Every instance of denial will stimulate further growth. Dolto (1984) compares this process with pruning young plants; the gardener knows that trimming will strengthen the roots and lead to a healthier plant. When a child is confronted with social limitations, she grows. The first reaction is one of disappointment at not getting what she wants, but at the same time she is challenged to take new steps. When the child is weaned and the maternal body as a source of food is denied, the child has learned to eat independently. The child acquires a position of her own in relation to the parent. She has learned to use her mouth to speak for herself. When the child flushes the toilet, she is learning that she cannot keep everything to herself. Similarly, the child learns that she cannot keep her mother for herself, and no longer acts as her mother's extension but acts from her own position. When the child is denied something, she gets words in return, and so acquires a subjective position with limited autonomy. By putting herself forward to speak, the child *subjects* herself to the language system. The child's narrative is formulated in a language that transcends the individual speaking. The child learns to say 'I', but when she says 'I' she is representing herself by means of a word rather than presenting an original self.

In order to function independently, the child has to acknowledge difference with other people. The child stops wanting to be everything for the other and acknowledges the separation from the other with whom she used to live in illusory unity. One can only want to be like the other if one can acknowledge the difference. The child now loses the 'immediacy of the imaginary positions' (Mooij, 1975). The child's exclusive access to the maternal body is prohibited, not only by the father but also by the mother's work and other activities. The child is holding out the prospect of other identifications with other persons and activities.

The child now becomes part of a community of other subjects who use a common system of symbols and a continuing interaction in which the subjects recognise each other. The symbolic position is conditional for developing faith in oneself and an internal locus of control, believing that outcomes are contingent on one's own responses rather than determined by fate, chance, luck or powerful others (Lefcourt, 1976). The child learns that social contracts rather than the use of force make a social life possible. It begins to see fellow citizens as different people with rights and obligations rather than rivals (Mooij, 2010). The transition from having the illusion of *being* the centre of the world to the awareness of *having* limited power is a delicate issue for the child.

The parents' task is now to help the child to cope in a positive way with this loss of power and to stimulate her to go into the world and to see what is so interesting about it and what makes them have more on their mind than solely the child. The child stops looking for her duplicate in the hope that they are just like her, but now wants to be *like* the others. Many social bonds may break into the exclusive parent–child relationship (Benjamin, 1990). The parent may have to go to work or have other children to look after. The essential thing is that the rules of the culture do not permit the child and parent to be everything to each other. The child's wish also to be part of a world to which the parent is attracted stimulates the child to address the outside world. The nature of relations to other people now becomes triangular: a relation to another who in turn relates to others rather than a one-to-one relationship.

Lacan (1958) explains that the child identifies with the 'name-of-the-father' rather than the father himself. Identification with him would exchange absolute dependency on the mother for absolute dependency on the father, and would only result in a change of power. The identification with the name-of-the-father means that the child is not permitted to do what the father does (with mother) (Mooij, 1985). The symbolic identification is the child's acknowledgement of the cultural rules, which helps the child to set herself free not only from the mother but from all imaginary relations (including those of the father). The child now becomes a subject with rights. The identification with the *name*-of-the-father also explains why the detachment process can occur when an actual father is absent in the child's life, since this absence does not imply that the rules no longer apply. The rules remain applicable and are represented by others. It is not so much the father as his name. It is the negative of the unspeakable tie with the mother, and the positive of the promising outside world. It connotes the mother's involvements with people other than the child. The name-of-the-father represents everything outside the dual relationship with the primary caregiver.

We have described the development of individual agency, the process of considering oneself as undivided, a centre of action, and the acknowledgment of having a limited position among other agents. This is a social process, meaning that the origin of the sense of 'I' and the becoming of a subject originate in the context of the individual. As Lacan (1958) says, the psyche is immersed in signification, children becoming subjects at the moment they start to speak and subject to the language system they use. Foucault (1979) claims that subjects are just the outcome of the exercise of power. This means that human agency and structure are inseparable, but they are not united. According to Giddens (1984), human agents are social knowledgeable actors rather than passive recipients of social forces. They have a will of their own and limited freedom to act and to change the course of events. Social structure is both the facility and the outcome of individual actions; people are socialised by social structures, but individual acts contribute to the development of these structures.

Broken individual agency

Transitions in the developmental process of becoming a human agent are delicate moments in which children are extra vulnerable to disturbances. The transition from the feeling of being united with the people and things around one, from a feeling of omnipotence, to an awareness of limited abilities is crucial. Yet this shift also comes at a moment when the child is still fragile and therefore has to be guided by those who take care of her. Dolto (1984) explains that if a young child's parent does not come home, because of an emergency admission to hospital, for instance, the child will wait for the parent to arrive. If, after a few weeks that parent returns home, the child expects to meet the same parent as some weeks before. It is hard for the child to connect the maintained image of the parent to the reality that has changed since then. Such an event may disturb the connection between body schedule and body image, causing the child difficulty in understanding the words spoken by that parent because she cannot relate them to the parent's physical reality. If the parent had no opportunity to maintain continuity with the child and to pass care for the child to someone known by the child, the child may no longer be able to make sense of the comforting words of the parent. Such interruptions of the relationship between image and schedule often have dramatic consequences for the child's psychological development and communicative capacities. The infant can deal with minor changes, as long as connecting traces remain in the memory.

Mental health problems develop when, at crucial developmental transitions, caregivers do not say comforting words to the child, or because the words that were spoken are not meant or are a lie: 'Ce qui traumatise, c'est le mensonge' (Dolto, 1994, p 90). The lie has a traumatising effect, because it does not convey the emotions that accompany the genuine spoken with conviction. If the child does not understand the words spoken, the relationship between body schedule and body image will disintegrate.

Mannoni (1967) presents a case previously analysed by Laing (1961) that explains what happens if a child is left by a mother who cannot express her emotions, hopes and expectations and therefore remains silent. Brian is a boy of four years of age who is presented for adoption by his mother. Mother cannot deal with the farewell, gives the child a kiss, breaks into tears and leaves without saying a word. Brian does not see his mother again and does not want to accept the adoptive adults as parents. Yet the adoptive parents consider Brian their son. Brian's behaviour becomes more and more disturbed. Laing notes that the boy now no longer knows who he is. He was the son of a mother, but he waits for her in vain and his adoptive parents regard him as *their* son. According to Mannoni, the trauma is caused by the familial ties between mother and child being broken and the child being removed from his family of origin without any explanation. The adoptive parents want Brian to be their son, but Brian's mother has made this transition impossible, because she did not explain to Brian that he was no longer her child. The child believes he has been rejected, because his mother was unable to tell him how terrible it was for her to leave him. The child does not understand why his mother could not take care of him. He complies with this rejection, because that is the body image that is presented to him: he must be a bad child. The adoptive parents have wiped out the child's past, they continue to respond at the level of the child's everyday behaviour and the child's needs are unconsciously neglected.

Disturbances of personal agency develop when primary caregivers are unable to structure the life of an infant. Unsteady caregivers probably have less capacity to acknowledge the child's separate agency and at the same time to let the child feel that he is safe and certain. If parents are barely able to run their own lives, the child may be an extra burden rather than a meaningful addition. If the parents use the child to escape daily misery, the child fulfils his parents' desire rather than being helped to develop his own desires. The most essential condition is that the parents should desire their child. The experience of being a wished-for child feeds the awareness that life has sense because it fulfils an important wish of the parent. If this basic experience is missing, the child will always lack a basic sense that life is worthwhile.

Disorders that develop during the first year often have a fundamental nature: the child failing to develop a solid self-image with an organising function. If the child has not identified, or has identified poorly, with a continuous image and as a consequence does not achieve a sense of coherence and self, he will maintain an imaginary structure in which the other is considered the same as the self; other people cannot be acknowledged as being different. The child cannot put himrself in the position of other people and real contact is difficult; the child feels at the mercy of other people and of the course of events. If the child is unable to structure his life with the help of a distinguishing self-image, he may lose interest in other people and things. Life then becomes a sequence of unrelated, isolated episodes, which results in fragmentary life narratives (Hoogenboezem,

2003). There is no horizon of meaning and sudden changes overwhelm the child, who sinks into an inner void. In other words, the child does not develop an internal locus of control and has little capacity to gear his own psychological capacities and needs to the wishes of other people. Often, such children try to create safety by resorting to routines that help them to structure their lives in a predictable way. The most serious problems occur when an excessive demand is made on structural capacities that in fact the child lacks. Life may then become so threatening that a flight from reality seems the only way out. Most children possess a huge capacity for finding their place in new circumstances, even when these have traumatising effects. Discontinuity only arises when children are no longer able to give meaning to new circumstances and as a result lose the sense of being one and the same person.

Less serious than psychotic disorders, but serious enough, are developmental disturbances that arise after a solid self-image has been constructed. An incomplete entrance into the symbolic position is the main cause of this kind of problem, and leads to difficulties in distancing the self in relation to the other. Mooij (2010) distinguishes three kinds of problem. *Compulsive* people want to keep others at a safe distance, for instance, by preventing others from asking questions by posing questions themselves. The desires of other people are considered to be ominous and therefore have to be neutralised. The price to be paid is the constant need of the compulsive person to disguise his or her subjectivity (because a clear presentation of that would provoke questions). This type of person longs for the impossible and wants constant proof that he or she cannot get what they want. On the contrary, the *hysteric* type does anything they can to draw the other's attention because their own desire is ignored (after all, the desire must be desired by the other). These people desire an unsatisfied desire (a repeated disappointment because their own imperfection cannot be accepted). In the *perverse* type, the desire of the other is denied and the aim is to compensate for that by being everything to the other. This type of person does not dare to separate and develop a desire of his or her own because the sex difference is not acknowledged. In these three types of pathology, people try to protect themselves against being different from the other. They often reason in an all-or-nothing fashion, and harbour the unrealistic expectation that they will be able to achieve absolute perfection; if that expectation is not met, their mood swings through 180 degrees and leaves them inconsolably unhappy.

Any developmental transition is a crisis in the sense that certain steps are necessary conditions for a healthy development. When a child enters the symbolic order, he is again subject to constraining influences. The discovery of difference and the limited capacity of subjective positions are essential to growth; it is an acknowledgement that one can never gain absolute power, something that most children previously thought possible. It is crucial that parents bar their children from everything that is no longer necessary for their development. This stimulates the child to seek his luck somewhere else and motivates him to discover the world. It gives him a subjective position, enabling him to become an autonomous person. Limitation is the basis of parental authority; as representatives of the law, they grant the child his own domain. In an ideal situation, this limitation is simultaneously a new perspective for the child ('authority' stems from the Latin *augere*, which means 'make grow'). Problems arise when the transition from omnipotence to limited subjectivity is disturbed. If the child is not restrained when limitations are necessary, the development of the child's subjectivity will be inhibited. As a result, he will have difficulty acknowledging his own limitations and those of others. This also happens when limitations are imposed, not as a consequence of the general rule, but in the personal interests of the caregiver. The child then has little possibility of setting himself free from the imprisoning desires of parents who will not let him go. Problems can also arise where parents are incapable of comforting the child in his loss of omnipotence or of pointing towards the new perspectives offered by the future; in such cases, the child will be disappointed by his apparent loss of total power and find it hard to take a comfortable position in relation to other people.

Such psychological disturbances stem from the fact that the child is barred from the symbolic structure rather than the result of real events. He cannot use the words that can help to make and maintain his own position. If parents do not allow their children to take up such an autonomous position and the desires that go with it, these children will always be 'partial objects' and will not succeed in developing agency of their own. As a result, such children need external agency and often have to rely on some kind of professional help. The more disturbed the individual agency, the more permanent the need for professional help. Sometimes, this support is found in a stable relationship in which not too intimate an appeal is made of the other person. In the main, however, these children need professional help with organising a stable and structured environment that gives them a permanent external locus of control.

Conclusion

Children are not born with a psychological core already primed and waiting to unfold. The baby is still beyond human society and is received and protected by the parents, who are the first representatives of that society. Little by little, the infant frees herself from her cocoon and turns to a human community, by identifying with the images presented and by speaking with the culture's symbols. These are the most important means by which the child constructs continuity, gives structure to her existence and conducts her life among other people. The child will only be able to free herself from the captivity of the imaginary once she can reach beyond the borders of her immediate material world. It is the symbolic system of language that enables the child to refer to absent situations – the past, the future and the world of other people. In the course of her life, the child acquires a more complex language that makes it possible to organise her life and take an independent position in relation to others. Development is a linguistic and social process.

The imaginary and symbolic positions so crucial to the child's development demand two types of parental reaction. For infants, it is crucial that the parents present a constant image and try as far as possible to prevent ruptures in the child's life. The infant is subject to a multiplicity of impressions and has to recognise patterns in these impressions in order to find coherence in her life; the almost unconditional love and almost unlimited attention given to the child provides a basic configuration of trust and certainty. The infant needs almost endless repetitions to instil a sense that its image coincides with its new psychological awareness of being one and the same – that he is 'really' John or that she is 'really' Mary. The child trusts blindly in what is said by people around her. The words spoken in welcome or to comfort the child are signs of reception and acceptance in human community. Hearing these words, the infant unquestioningly accepts that her place is with her parents and in the world they represent. Children who do not hear these words of acceptance, will (often) miss this unquestioning trust in themselves (internal locus of control) and feel the permanent need to look for this elsewhere.

In the symbolic position, on the other hand, the parents need to limit their child. The child has to know her place in the world, which implies limitation. A major contribution of parents here is to give words to life's boundaries and to what is lost and what is prohibited. With the entry into language, the child commits herself to the social limitations and the limited position of belonging in a community with other people who are subject to the same laws. The parental role is to give the child maximum space within these limits, a life that is *motivated* by personal desires and *limited* by the desires of other people.

The imaginary and symbolic positions are crucial for the development of basic psychological structures. Fundamental though these positions are, they are open to change and differentiation. Children grow up in a communicative context and intrapersonal and interpersonal processes lead to a complex interaction of individual and social influences in which the child learns through interaction. To make herself intelligible, both to others and to herself, a child has to use the symbols provided by a common cultural basis. A recognisable self that can resist permanent changes in body and environment becomes an agency that is approachable (with a name) and responsible.

The dialogical nature of both individual personality and human organisations is a major theme in this book. Changes, shifts and ruptures are a necessary condition for individual development and, at both this level and the level of social organisation, dialogue is an essential pre-condition for change. Discontinuity only arises when an individual is unable to give new facts, events and experiences a place in his or her symbolic system or cannot change that system to accommodate these phenomena in meaningful positions. When this happens, the relationship between the physical scheme and the psychic image of the body gets disturbed; new words have to be found to restore continuity. This is not to say that all damage is repairable. Rather, the person tries to find new words to verbalise his or her life situation in different words. If, however, the words found do not prevent damage, there is discontinuity, and development is disturbed. This may lead to a conception of life as a series of unconnected fragments. Dialogue is the very instrument needed to regain continuity and to gain a new sense of meaning and meaningfulness. But even dialogue is not always a sufficient remedy; words alone cannot always succeed in restoring order to dysfunctional lives. Some people will always be dependent on the structure provided by their environment. Although in this book dialogue is advocated as the crucial means of assisting clients of welfare, every society must also provide for its children the human structures that they cannot organise for themselves.

THREE

Social interaction and interactive agency

The single biggest problem in communication is the illusion that it
has taken place.
George Bernard Shaw

Chapter Two explains how a child's individual agency develops through interaction
with its caretakers. Later chapters will explore how social agency develops as a
result of social structures, but this chapter focuses on agency as an element of
human interaction. Social interaction is where intrapersonal processes intersect
with social structures; it is influenced by the characters of those who are involved
in the communication and by the social categories that shape its context. But
both personality and social structures are in turn shaped by social interactions;
there is a process of mutual interaction involving intrapersonal, interpersonal and
macro social processes (Coté and Levine, 2002; Verkuyten, 2005).

Social interactions have a dynamic of their own, which is discussed in this
chapter. Agency at an interactional level is about the voice of the participants being
heard, about their contribution to the exchange of thoughts in encounters, and
about their capacity to present and negotiate identities. Interacting agents are in a
process of permanent transformation. As explored in Chapter One, 'agency' refers
to an individual's ability to actively take position in different times and locations,
without losing a personal, stabilising anchor that makes continuity possible and
acknowledges the boundaries of the self and others. 'Interactive agency' refers
to a performative capacity to act with a certain degree of autonomy and to take
position in relation to other people. It goes with both the protection of one's
personal integrity and respect for the other's boundaries.

Becoming an agent in communication is a learning process. Children are trained
to become active agents when they are addressed as participants, as individuals
who make a difference. Interactive agency is developed by the appeal to a moral
position rather than simply by acquiring communicative skills or interactive
competencies. Developing communicative agency means learning to consider
how to act in the right way in variable situations. This means not only a correct
orientation toward external norms but also the ability to refer to internalised
norms (Sokol et al, 2004).

The development of agency is a process of gaining and building trust in social
relations, developing social responsibility and gradually becoming familiar with
social manners. In general, children's voices have become louder in modern family
life, but this is not the case in all families. There are great differences between

cultures, both within and between societies, in the level of interactive agency attained by children. These differences are the result of differences in skills that are related to the social conditions in which children grow up. In addition, (sub) cultures differ in their norms about the desirable level of autonomy for children.

Developing interactive agency

The communicative context in which children grow up is crucial for the development of their interactional potentialities. The social context may change, but it also contains stable elements that enable the child to develop a recognisable social position. The responsive qualities of parents are crucial for interactive agency to grow. Parents give their children the illusion that they (the parents) have a grip on the world and create a safe environment in which their children are held emotionally and physically. This gives them a glimpse of a world they can trust sufficiently to enter on their own (Winnicott, 1965).

In communication through language, people give meaning to life. This is an interactive process, as people learn about themselves in contrast to others. Vygotsky suggests that human mental functions are of a dialogical nature and that in development, monologues appear later than dialogues. Children's thought is the internalisation of external dialogues, external speech becoming internal (Vygotsky, 1978). Children's abilities of self-organisation are built on talk with others in which children develop a capacity to play the language games of their community (Wertsch, 2008). Martin (2006) emphasises, in his interpretation of Mead's theory of perspectives, that agency is a self-interpreting reaction to the perspectives of the social situation the person is absorbed in, rather than an internalisation of the perspectives of others. The growth of agency is again considered as a relational rather than a mental development. Positions taken in external dialogues become conversations between internal 'I' positions (Hermans and van Kempen, 1993), the child internalising the conversational roles of both speaker and listener. Agency is more than 'Me' because it also contains a reaction to the 'Me', one that may become increasingly self-interpretive with repeated and differentiated experiences, especially in problem-solving situations.

In presenting themselves, children are guided by the dominant categories of identity of the cultural context in which they grow up. If they are well informed, children learn how to behave according to the conventions and develop the skills to do so. They learn to control the impressions they make. Most of these skills are developed in interaction with primary caregivers. Through participation in instructive communication with parents and other caregivers, children learn all kinds of (verbal) skills that help them to function at an independent level. This learning process may be considered as the transfer of competences by others to an independent, internal, coordinating mechanism. Caregivers provide scaffolding for an infant when she cannot (yet) function on her own (Wood, 1988). They surround the child with a supportive system that structures the child's behaviour; they instruct performances precisely and check to ensure that the child can manage without their help. If the parents are successful, a bit of the scaffold will be removed; if not, they will refine their instruction. 'Scaffolding' may be a confusing term, as it seems to put emphasis on the adult's initiatives and neglects the child's activities, yet children learn to act individually by interacting and appropriating what is jointly produced (Rogoff et al, 2003). Strategies that are modelled by the adults as interpersonal strategies during the interaction are internalised by children as their own individual cognitive strategies. Children thus play an active role in the transition from interpersonal to intrapersonal functioning, as novices who want to learn and achieve more control over their life (Hoogsteder, 1995). External dialogues are internalised in a continuing dynamic in which interpersonal and intrapersonal processes are linked (Hermans, 2001), and which may result in positional shifts in relation to other people and the environment (Harré and van Langenhove, 1991). The stories we tell about ourselves in some sense construct who we are (Redman, 2005). Narrative performances are influenced by the nature of the communicative context in which certain narrative structures (linearity and continuity) are better accepted than others. What are the contextual conditions in which children are raised and how do these contribute to an interactive agency?

The dialogical character of developmental context

From the very outset, parents communicate with their infants and speak to them as communicative partners (Bertau, 2004). Because their lives are still fragmented and lack an elementary meaning, young children are dependent on their parents for achieving a sense of continuity. The meaning the child's caregivers attach to the child's activities determines the child's understanding and experience. Babies already recognise smells, sounds and sights, but the parents determine the way in which these become memories. The baby does not initially develop a position of her 'own', but is rather enveloped by parental nurturing. The baby is caught in a repeating pattern set by the same caregiver(s), who, in a strict timetable, feed her and address her by the same name. The quality of a child's identity depends on the continuity and reliability of the context in which she grows up. If the parents speak lovingly to the child, she will learn that this developing self is a continuous and reliable basis. In this way, she gradually builds a complex system of recognition, detection and awareness that enables her to organise her life amid permanently changing circumstances. In other words, the child will develop interactive agency, the ability and confidence to start and continue communicating with people around her.

Envelopment is followed by *development*. A young child who have grown up in a loving environment will eventually have to acknowledge that the world does not revolve around her; her caregivers are busy with their own affairs and their desires extend to other people as well as to the child. The child has to accept her limited capacity to draw attention and must learn to stand on her own. The social context thus plays an important initiatory and facilitating role in the child's ability to develop an organising capacity. She needs a stable environment to discover continuity, but she also needs change and diversity to learn about the boundaries of self and others.

Development is not merely the internalisation of norms and skills presented by adults, but rather a dialogical and transactional process with both parents and children taking an active role. The conventional view is that children learn by the transmission of knowledge from the adult to the child, whereby the adult actively presents the knowledge and the child passively receives the information. From a dialogical point of view, however, it is rather a transactional and transformative process in which both adult and child construct new meanings and change during the process (Polman and Pea, 2001). Development is a communicative process. From the very first weeks of life, the dialogical character of the relationship between parents and their newborn children is observable, as the emotional state of the parent affects the child and vice versa (Trevarthen, 1979). To use the example from Chapter Two, even when the mother goes to post a letter, she tries to organise her child's life by talking to her. Although she knows that her child cannot understand the meaning of her words, she nevertheless assumes that she can reassure the child through the words directed at her. The dialogue is a pattern the child may use to structure her own life.

A major step in this process is the child's learning to engage the attention of a social partner and coordinate it with her own focus. The child becomes skilled at drawing someone else's attention to an object in order to share an awareness of it (Mundy and Gomes, 1997). The parent's role is to engage the child in social sharing activities (Garner et al, 1996) and to guide the child in participating (Rogoff, 1990), transforming the use of symbols (Adamson et al, 2005). Children learn through interaction with others and perform in company what they cannot yet do on their own. Developing interactive agency means creating and maintaining intersubjectivity, that is, children have to transcend their private worlds and, with the help of language, create a common world (Rommetveit and Blakar, 1979).

From the parents' point of view, supporting their child to acquire individual agency seems to be a contradictory enterprise. Larson (2006) refers to this as 'intentionality paradox'. On the one hand, adults have the intention of guiding young people and protecting them against all kind of social dangers; on the other hand, they try to give them space to develop an experience of intentionality themselves. Parenting is seeking a middle course, respecting the individual direction in which their child wants to go and showing an interest in her intentions, but at the same time warning the child against the risks of certain objectives and even preventing her from taking these risks.

Identity work

Interactive agency has a narrative and a performative nature; the stories people tell construct who they are and these stories are always presentations of self in a particular context. This is where social structure and individual performance meet. Narrative identity is both the repetition of former practices and the externalisation of personal intentions, carried out in a specific social context. In these contexts, some narrative structures are preferred to others; in western cultures, for instance, linearity, coherence, causality and continuity are the preferred narrative values. Verbal and non-verbal interaction is conditional for negotiating roles and mutual adaptation (Goffman, 1981). A constructivist view presupposes that different visions of reality may exist side by side, but accepts the dominance of particular 'scripts' of life.

As discussed in Chapter Two, each individual presents reality through images and symbols. This is always an imperfect performance, as the individual cannot represent himself or herself completely in and through the language that he or she speaks; the word 'I' can never fully represent the self. Anything that people say about themselves is incomplete; there is always something left unsaid. Yet these narratives are a vital condition for developing identity, as they create niches in which provisional coherence may be constructed. Narratives are hybrid efforts, attempts to hold the person together by summoning overlapping but independent positions (Dawson, cited in Redman, 2005). People develop their identity in the social field that other people also enter with their own self-presentations.

Goffman's (1959) theory of the dramaturgical character of human behaviour in social situations was a landmark in the thinking about the development of the interactive self. People play roles and present themselves to others in the stories they tell and the way they 'act'. The roles one plays become second nature, as people start believing in them and become 'engrossed' (Goffman, 1974). The impression one wants to make is often idealised and presents a more favourable image of the role player. People expect others to value and treat them according to the type of person they present. This is not always a perfect fit, but in most daily interactions people will try to agree on (temporary) definitions that will prevent open conflicts. Individuals present an implicit definition of who they are and how they want to be approached by others. This is a moral demand, the individual expecting from others to be treated in a way that belongs to the kind of person that is presented. People do their best to give a favourable impression of themselves so that people think highly of them. They do that by expressing themselves in such a way as to give other people 'the kind of impression that will lead to act voluntarily in accordance with his own plans' (Goffman, 1959, p 4). But the individual can never be sure that his or her dramatic work is sufficiently convincing, for the audience evaluation will always take into account other elements than those intended in the dramatic presentation of the person's identity. Impressions are created both consciously and unconsciously (Chaiken and Trope, 1999), so there is no absolute control over the impression that is conveyed. Again, the impression one gives of one's identity is imperfect. After all, the presentation itself will immediately alter the presenter's identity. The impression one wants to make needs permanent maintenance without revealing to the audience the energy that it costs to play the role. Communication, however, is an interactive process rather than two solo performances and only in extreme situations is it controlled by only one of the partners. All kinds of cues may be given unintentionally and lead to misunderstandings, but, according to Goffman, performers usually try to mitigate the effect of these and underline impressions that are 'compatible and consistent with the over-all definition of the situation that is being fostered' (1959, p 51). Intentionally or not, in the presentation of identities in daily interactions, the reality content of these presentations will never be fully revealed. There is never a clear distinction between reality and pretence; there are merely multiple perspectives on realities. What we observe as real life is a dramatisation of it; life is a theatre (Goffman, 1974).

The development of interactive agency is a two-way process between individual and society. From a constructivist point of view, there can be no fundamental division between self and culture. Rather, agencies are shaped in a transactional process; the social context opens all kinds of potential activities for the individual person and the person in the end acts in a certain way, creating a new social context. The individual presents himself by accounting, explaining and justifying before an audience that is also involved, accepting or refusing particular elements of the narrative. Many social scientists reject a dualist view of the relationship between individual and society and approach it as a process either from inside-out or outside-in (Bruner, 1990). Agency comes into being in a dialogical process in which people take different positions towards each other and produce new meaning, trying to find shared understanding and common ground. The self is presented in these dialogues and reproduced by each representation. It is 'a multiplicity of spaces, cavities, relations, divisions established through a kind of in-folding of exteriority' (Rose, 1996b, p 300).

Coming of age in this world means being able to negotiate with other people, to reflect on the self and to 'manage impressions'. These skills demand specific communicative capacities. Western societies demand a high level of mediated interaction with an emphasis on visibility, resulting in a decentred self in 'an endless play of signs that shift with every movement' (Thompson, 1995). In such rapidly changing social conditions, people have to be able to quickly read and understand messages and to react to them, to adapt their communicative style to changing requirements, to be able to put aside personal feelings and present a socially acceptable face. As more and more emphasis has been put on people's self-realisation, the standards for these individual capacities also have become higher. Intercultural communication between people who come from high-context cultures (Hall, 1976) and people who use little contextual information is often problematic. People from high-context cultures are oriented towards each other's background, and often communicate indirectly, aiming at establishing harmony and preventing loss of face in the encounter (Ting-Toomey and Oetzel, 2002). A low-context culture, on the other hand, is characterised by short-term relationships and the style of communication is accordingly straightforward and explicit. A disparity in this regard between interlocutors may easily lead to different role expectations, with western-oriented citizens paying less attention to formal communicative conventions than immigrant citizens. Ignorance of conversational conventions may result in withdrawing from conversation as a way of reducing uncertainty about how to behave and how to understand what the other means (Gudykunst and Kim, 2003; Samovar et al, 2006. Anxiety caused by the different approach of someone from a different culture makes it difficult to understand or sympathise with the other's attitudes and feelings and militates against effective communication (Gudykunst and Nishida, 2001).

Broken interactive agency

Mental disturbances can lead to pathological communication, for instance in verbal distortions. According to the theory of pragmatic communication, there is a good chance that people who are chronically exposed to the pathogenic aspects of double-bind relationships become schizophrenic. In a double-bind relationship, the victim gets an order that cannot be carried out and at the same time is barred from the meta-communication that would allow the possibility of talking about the paradoxical character of the order. Time and again, the victim is invited to take a certain social position and then has to acknowledge that this position is undermined. In the end, there is only one way out for the victim and that is to withdraw from interaction with other people and from daily reality. The schizophrenic has lost grip on reality, in the sense that he or she no longer believes that other people share his or her views on reality. The victim confuses reality and fantasy, because the basis of subjectivity has been lost. Although there is often a kind of coherence in the stories the victim tells, other people will find them incoherent and incomprehensible. Rommetveit (1974, pp 53-4) illustrates this with a case of a schizophrenic patient who gives his account of a party: "I too was invited, I went to the ball … and it rolled and rolled away". The man wants to tell his interlocutor that he went to a party and explain what happened there. Once he has spoken the word 'ball', however, the conversation flags and the course of the story deviates from the man's originally intended story – and from the listener's expectations (that he would find out what happened at the ball). The patient gets confused over what he has just said and tries to catch the last word he uttered, but he has lost the context of the start of the conversation when he still had common ground with the conversational partner. Now the patient's problem is how to explain that last word to people from a different world and without a common frame of reference. The continuation of the sentence ("and it rolled and rolled away") is a solution to this new conversational problem because it fits with a common meaning of the word 'ball' in the sense of an object for sport and games. This interpretation is not unreasonable, if one starts from the premise that the speaker wants to make sense but is evidently insensitive to how the story will be received by the listener. How to end the story? It is a gamble, but he chooses the option that, for him, has the best chance.

Meaningful communication is only possible if people believe that their perception of reality is shared by other people; this is known as intersubjectivity, when one listens to someone else and tries to understand what has been said. When perceptions of reality are shared, communication enhances people's grasp on their own lives. The situation of the schizophrenic, on the other hand, is characterised by alienation and the inability to move easily within this domain of intersubjectivity. When the listener tries to understand what his interlocutor has said, he starts from the assumption that what has been said conforms to what they both take to be common knowledge. Thus, in general, verbal communication is a mutual and complementary contract. From one aspect, there is an encoding based on the idea that what one says itself assumes – and is aimed at – shared understanding. At the receiver's end, decoding is an effort to reconstruct what the speaker *meant* to say. The 'mistake' of schizophrenics is that they are, throughout the exchange, self-oriented rather than imagining themselves in the position of the listener. In earlier life, the schizophrenic has been unable to develop the interactive agency that would have created a moment of intersubjectivity in his interaction with other people. Most human interactions are based on the assumption that common knowledge and shared understanding may be achieved; we constantly move between the position of speaker and the position of listener to produce maximal intersubjectivity. People with poor interactive agency, however, lack the steady communicative base that is a prerequisite to starting relationships with others.

Other interactive disorders may be prevalent in children and adolescents. Children who have been confronted with serious threats in their early lives may lack the internal locus of control necessary to engage in open communication with others. Studies show a positive correlation between external locus of control and maladjustment, including high anxiety and depression (Kliewer and Sandler, 1992). It is precisely the intimacy that other people enjoy when they become familiar with their interlocutors that horrifies them, because they have learned to associate such familiarity with danger. Whenever they experience a cautious desire for intimacy, it is at once extinguished, overwhelmed by the huge anxiety aroused by the possibility of a real relationship. The child abandons a meaningful dialogue. The social situation is experienced as so threatening that the child quits and drops back into the familiar dungeon of loneliness (Dolto, 1984).

The development of interactive agency is inevitably influenced by societal changes. Western societies may encourage the self-realisation of their citizens, but their economic and political structures appear to result in an emptiness of the self, accompanied by a chronic need to fill this vacancy by food, consumables and celebrities (Taylor, 1989). The bombardment by a mix of images makes high demands on individual psychological capacities, and inhibits symbolisation rather than encourages the acceptance of individual differences which is necessary for starting and maintaining meaningful relationships (Žižek, 1991; Bendle, 2002). These contemporary social conditions promote the development of the 'longing personality', which, as the result of 'chronic perceptual poverty', suffers from a constant need for fulfilment and an insatiable thirst for new experiences (Mooij, 2010). The first two chapters of this book describe how emptiness is the starting point for all human beings and how humans are constantly creating imaginary and symbolic identifications in an effort to escape this emptiness.

The dominance of television and internet images undermines the capacity for reflection and the moral demands associated with symbolic processes. The predominance of fleeting images undermines the stability of the separation between the subject and the other, making the subject more vulnerable. This may be the cause of an increase in the number of people with borderline personalities, with their diffusion of identity and tendency to show extreme loyalty towards the other or the group. It may also lead to narcissistic personality disorders; when the subjective position is undermined, the other-image assumes such significance that the person reacts by trying to restore his or her self-image (Mooij, 2010).

At first sight, it may seem that some aspects of modern society favour people with such personality disorders. People who have difficulty with intimacy may profit from new communications technology that enables one-to-one contact at a distance. The modern human has a multi-voiced personality and is called on to deal with appeals to various aspects of the personality in different situations. With frequently changing constellations of people there seems to be ever more opportunity to avoid intimacy and concomitantly fewer chances for anxiety to arise.

Take Jennifer from our case study. She has a huge network of internet friends and is in contact with them almost every day. She likes to talk at a distance and shares some of her thoughts with her friends, parents and foster parents. It does not bring her close friendships with friends as she does not have intimate friends with whom she undertakes common activities.

In fact, this type of borderline personality disorder is not all suited to a multifaceted society. The person with multiple personality disorder has no free choice and is not like the individual who can assume different 'I' positions and who is capable of using these positions in different situations. On the contrary, the person with multiple personality disorder is at the mercy of external control mechanisms and will be thrown back and forth in rapidly changing conditions. Such a personality is in no way ideal for the modern man or woman. Modern society demands that individuals adopt different positions that may be interrelated and may lead to shifts (compare Barker and Galanski, 2001). There is a great difference between the person who *suffers* from a multiple personality disorder and the person who can *play* simultaneously with different aspects of his or her personality. The latter is able to pretend to be someone and then someone else, but is never afraid to lose himself or herself in these versions. The many selves imagined on the computer screen are different versions of the self that are chosen by an individual rooted in an overarching and stabilising formation. The person with multiple personality disorder lacks such a meta-position. For these people it is much harder to negotiate the quality of relationships in a self-confident way (Žižek, 1992). They tend to see those other people as a threat.

Poor professional agency

In the section above, I have presented the worst-case scenario in the development of interactive agency: developmental processes that have been deeply disturbed and have resulted in loss of a sense of reality and serious psychiatric syndromes. There are many psycho-social problems that affect interactive agency in a less drastic way. For several reasons, people may have difficulty in understanding another person's perspective and fail to reach a shared understanding in their communications with one another. As discussed in the last chapter, an incomplete entry into the symbolic order may cause problems for individuals in relating to the other. Other people may be perceived from the very start as threatening and upsetting, requiring permanent efforts to prevent them from being perceived as dangerous. The consequence is a pattern of communication in which the individual is focused more on neutralising the other than on presenting himself or herself. Another problem may arise when the subjectivity of the partner in communication is ignored and the individual needs to attract all the attention, or is constantly busy trying to satisfy the supposed needs of the other. Beside these psycho-social problems, intellectual disability may affect interactive agency and result in people missing the point of discussions, having difficulty in understanding jokes or not being able to reflect on their situation.

As discussed earlier, interactive agency arises at the intersection of individual and social processes. Hence, to understand disturbances in interactive agency, it is not enough to look exclusively at individual factors; the communicative context should also be considered. The various contexts in which people talk with each other create different communicative conditions. Everyday conversations are totally different from institutional talks, which are (institutional-) goal-oriented and are consequently often more formal and hierarchical (Drew and Heritage, 1995). Child welfare workers often find themselves in conversational situations that are neither wholly one nor the other. Their efforts to involve parents in discussions about family problems can be seen as an empowering strategy, but because their communication has specific institutional goals, their efforts also serve to reduce a client's opposition and may therefore be seen as a strategy to improve the efficiency of the process (Hofstede et al, 2001). In institutional communication in child welfare, professionals have to play a double role – in both care and control. The controlling aspect of child welfare workers' responsibilities requires them to collect reliable information about the relevant factors influencing the child's well-being; whereas their caring role demands that they help the parents reorganise their family. The two goals are often in conflict and at best make the position of professionals and clients ambiguous. This ambiguity is the reason why clients and child welfare workers spend so much time clarifying their roles and negotiating about formulations in official documents (van Nijnatten, 2006b). Institutional communication thus often ends in a sophisticated role play that makes great demands on the client's communicative competence. Clients who are not trained in this kind of interaction and are not accustomed to professional styles of reasoning will find themselves at a disadvantage in child welfare communication.

This is shown in the following two extracts from a case study (van Nijnatten, 2010). In this case, poor interactive agency is the result of an intimidating communicative context rather than cognitive or affective disturbances. The case concerns an encounter between two Dutch child welfare workers and a father in the context of a family supervision order. Just before the conversation cited in the extract below, the family supervisor explained, in a rather abstract way, why two supervisors were involved in the case.

In the extract, one of the family supervisors (FS1) mentions a written directive, which is the supervisor's power to assign a task to the parents, against which the latter may lodge an appeal. Although this is quite a technical aspect of the family supervision procedure, the family supervisor does not explain it in technical terms, but immediately cites an example, which concerns the second family supervisor (Caroline, FSC) discovering that the school the child is attending is not a good one. The family supervisor and the parents then get into a dispute over the choice of school:

1. FS1: 'Yes, again I stress that because it is <u>related</u> to what I just said. It is <u>not without its obligations</u> ... so it is not like, well, I will give you an example: Caroline finds out that one of the children attends a school that in our opinion is not good for him and then we start ... there's an investigation and the outcome is that another school would be better. This child simply has another level and it would be better off at this or that school. And then you say, for instance, that it is so far away and I don't like that at all.'

2. Father: 'Doesn't the teacher decide that?'

3. FS1: 'Well, the <u>teacher</u> sees the child and he also will give <u>advice</u> about that and that's why Caroline was just saying that it is so important to keep in touch with the teacher. The point is that the teacher gives this advice and the teacher can then say he ought to go to that school but he cannot decide that, in the end *you* are the one who has authority over the children so <u>you can</u> say what you want. But at the moment, because of the child protection measure, you have to share this authority with the family guardian, so that <u>in fact</u>, at the moment, we <u>together</u> are the boss //over the children //' 4. Father: // yes but // if I go to school ...'

5. FS1: 'Yes ...'

6. Father: '... and I have a talk with the teacher ...'

7. FS1: 'Yes ...'

8. Father:'… and I hear all this … then he asks me if I agree with it …'

9. FS1:'… and if you then say, I don't agree … then the teacher can<u>not</u> just say I will place him in another school anyway, but in the case of a family supervision order I, the <u>family supervisor</u>, am also involved in this and then we will talk and if you then say I don't agree …'

10. Father:'Why should I disagree? If the teacher thinks it's a good idea …'

11. FS1:'Yes, I don't know.'

12. Father:'He is doing his job, isn't he?'

13. FSC:'But there can be all kind of reasons. It could be that you, say, help will cost, money, or it could be that it is too far away and that's why you disagree, or that you think, I won't do that because then every morning my wife has to take the child a long way and that will be too much trouble, we won't do that. And then <u>Helen</u> might decide, listen Mr K [father], that may be so but it's in the best interests of the child, heh, I call it for his development, that's what we were just talking about.'

14. Father: No, [now you are] talking about the best interests of my <u>wife</u>.'

15. FSC:'No, because it would be in the best interest of the child to go to another school.'

16. Father:'Yes, but all the same you are talking about the best interests of my <u>wife</u>.'

The result of the family supervisor's explanation is confusion, with father disputing the example rather than bothering about the written directive. The explanation is hard to follow; although the family supervisor says she will give an example, the description is very realistic and formulated in the present tense. Instead of saying, "Imagine that Caroline thinks the school is no good", the family supervisor says, "Caroline finds out that one of the children attends a school that in our opinion is not good for him". This realistic description of the 'example' is maintained. It is said that the teacher will give advice (3). The mix-up of active and present tense ("he will give advice") may confuse the father, since it can easily be understood as something that the is actually doing. The explanation is immediately followed by a meta-remark indicating the relevance of this advice. It is alleged that parents have the last word, but not in the case of a family supervision order. In the following exchanges, it appears that the father does not take the example as one of a category of cases of dispute between family supervisor and clients, but rather as an indication of a concrete difference of opinion: if the teacher were to tell him all this, the father would have no reason to disagree. Why should he? (10). Now the family supervisor seems to be confused (11) and falls silent. The father justifies his point by referring to the teacher's professionalism ("doing his job"). Caroline says that he might have several reasons to disagree (13). Her language is again layered; moreover, she is referring to what her colleague previously said, which makes it harder for father to react. The father seems to misinterpret Caroline's remark as a plea to consider the interests of the mother. Caroline repeats that the child's interest would be best served by sending her to the other school (15). The father sticks to his point and repeats his view that they would agree with whatever in the teacher's view would be of what is in the best interests of their child. This goes on for some time, at the end of which the family supervisor concludes:

> 65. FS1: 'Then you just say, I'm the father and I'm the boss.... And what I want to explain to you is that with a family supervision you are the father and you are the boss ... and I am the family supervisor and together we are the boss [FSC writes something down] and we have to decide together, like what school the child should attend. And if I then ... eh, if I say the child should go to this or that school in K, then that's rather stronger than advice, in fact that's an order and if we couldn't work it out, well then perhaps we would have to see whether the juvenile judge, so to speak.'

> 66. Father: 'But that would be to the child's advantage, wouldn't it?'

> 67. FSC: 'Mmm.'

> 68. FS1: 'Fine. I think if we explain it that way and you understand it then maybe we can cooperate very well, for then you are indeed thinking very much about the best interests of the child and not about the interests of your wife, because she has to walk further, you see?'

The conclusion, that the father's extra comments make it possible to reach mutual understanding, is rather self-serving. One might rather say that the father, in spite of the supervisors, has managed to convince them that he is acting in the best interests of his children. The family supervisor almost formulates this as their own discovery ("'indeed'"), whereas in fact, it was their own stereotypical presupposition rather than the father's actual remarks that had *prevented* them from realising this earlier.

The family supervisors talk in complex and layered speech in their attempt to bring the father to a more general and distanced position from which he might look differently at his family problems. When the father declines to follow, the encounter becomes bogged down in a repetitious explanation of bureaucratic tasks, legal rules and professional intentions. This professional power play is amplified by the fact that two supervisors are talking to one parent (most of the time). On several occasions, the family supervisors point out to the father that they have the legal power and that he is obliged to cooperate. It is no wonder then that the father resorts to reporting concrete facts. He often takes the supervisor's statements as concrete indications and does not react to their exemplary meaning; he takes the role of a responsible parent rather than of a client who wants to be informed about agency policies, legal details and procedures.

This is a typical example of institutional communication in which the differences in interactive agency between professional and client are obvious. It is impossible to establish whether the communicative misunderstandings are due to a lack of communicative skills on the part of the father or perhaps his poor cognitive capacities. But it is clear that the professional terminology is much too specialised and formulated in far too complex a way for the client to understand. Although the father defends himself rather well, there is irritation on both sides about the misunderstandings, all to the disadvantage of the child who might profit most from an intelligible communication leading to the necessary decisions.

Communication with children

Let us return to our case study, Jennifer, who has to attend a case conference. She is already angry before the meeting begins. She hates this kind of event, but she has prepared herself and has promised herself that she will stay calm. The case manager from the child welfare agency is present at the meeting as well as her mentor and foster mother. There are two points to discuss: her progress in holding a proper conversation and in building a social network. Jennifer thinks she is doing fine; she is popular in the lodge and during the weekends she often goes into town with one of the other girls. She is convinced that she has attained the goals set, but the other three think differently. For half an hour, they discuss the relevance of Jennifer making friends outside the lodge and they try to convince her to attend a sports club in order to make new friends, but she declines to do so. When they press the point, the only way for her to keep calm is to look out of the window and to withdraw from the conference. When the case manager says it is clear that she has not yet attained her goal of being able to hold a proper conversation, she explodes.

Whether and how children communicate with others depends not only on their individual skills but also on the social context in which the communication takes place. Children's interactive agency depends on their interpretation of the social context in which they communicate with others rather than merely the objective characteristics of such a communicative situation. This is demonstrated in a study of 'the inner logic' of foster children by Singer and colleagues (2004). The results of this study show that foster children dare to force their will on their parents less often than birth children, out of fear of the possible consequences.

Birth children are more certain that no matter what they say or do, their parents will still love them. Foster children appear to be less certain about the outcomes of relational disputes, having had bad experiences with their parents. Birth children start from the idea that their existence is not related to choice, whereas foster children may ask themselves why their own parents made the choice to hand over their child or were forced to let the child grow up in a different family. They are uncertain about whether their foster parent will back out of the decision they made to take them in. The situations in which children grow up differ greatly in terms of opportunities for communication, as does children's confidence that their attempts at communication will be understood, acknowledged and dealt with sympathetically. If children are uncertain about their psychological and social context, they may find it more difficult to enter into a sincere and faithful dialogue with others.

Traditionally, children were excluded from all kinds of communications related to their welfare. Very few parents would tell their children about an impending divorce; children were told fairy tales about sex and procreation and were kept away from dying people. Professionals also exercise restraint in approaching children as serious conversational partners. In institutional communication, young children in particular are often still considered as vulnerable being or victims to be protected, and many professionals have very little idea about how to approach children, what to tell them and how to ask questions of them. In a study of child welfare policy in cases of uxoricide, in very few cases were children briefed or debriefed by social workers from the Child Protection Board (van Nijnatten and van Huizen, 2004). The social workers thought it better not to tell them what had happened; the truth was considered too cruel for the children to deal with, even though nowadays most therapeutic experts recommend debriefing children after they have witnessed domestic violence (see, for example, Sudermann and Jaffe, 1997). Even when the children had been present in the room next to the scene of murder and had heard the screaming, they were not told what had happened. Yet it is crucial for children to hear what adults have to say about what has happened and there are no good psychological reasons for withholding from children the facts of such important events on the grounds that they will not be able to deal with them (Skolnick, 1973).

Children do not suffer less if they are not told the truth in such circumstances and the same goes for children of divorcing parents. Withholding information from them about the planned break-up, the reasons for the divorce, the post-divorce arrangements and so on only leads them to make up stories about what has happened and provokes them to seek the truth for themselves (Dolto, 1988b). Dolto (1988a) argues strongly in favour of openness and honesty towards children. If children are told the truth about their situation, for instance, about their real parentage, the whereabouts of their father (if he is in prison) or the results of a medical investigation, they acquire the tools they need to define their position and thus deal with the situation.

Nowadays, it is more common to acknowledge children as partners in communication, and this certainly makes it easier for them to develop interactive agency. Yet this is not always the case and in many social situations, both inside and outside families, children are still not recognised as persons in their own right who need to be addressed as partners. Children's new agency also brings new (moral) responsibilities. Kaganas and Diduck (2004) analyse how, in the divorce discourse, children may be cast as morally responsible victims who have to live up to the new ideals of the post-divorce child. Children are acknowledged as autonomous persons by having their original moral agency recognised (Tappan, 1997) rather than being guaranteed rights of self-determination. Too willing attention from adults may hinder the child in finding a position of its own. It is crucial that adults listen to children's points of view before stating their own. Children benefit most from participatory structures at school and in children's homes, and by being treated as fellow citizens who are heard by adults (de Winter, 1997). This is, of course, a social rather than a legal claim.

Conclusion

Interactive agency is the ability of an individual to take part in all kinds of daily social interactions. To estimate the degree of interactive agency a person has, it is necessary to take into account how a person usually acts in relevant communicative situations, the type of communications in which he or she is frequently involved and how that person operates in those interactions. Interactive agency is influenced by both personal and structural features. Children have to acquire various communicative skills to develop interactive competency. They do so early in life in interaction with their primary caregivers and other people. In these interactions, children not only learn about the world; they also learn about other people and about themselves. When they are given the opportunity, they become skilled at taking the initiative in encounters with others, presenting themselves according to social conventions and reflecting on their social performance.

Different cultures demand different interactive skills and in contemporary western societies these demands are changing at an unprecedented rate. This may add to a division between citizens who enjoy communicative privilege and those who are underprivileged. Citizens in these rapidly changing societies have to adapt to the various modes of communication and be assertive and open-minded. At the same time, they have fewer social structures to fall back on. People who come from high-context societies have more difficulty in keeping their footing in open and egalitarian modes of communication and in the end have to rely on collective agencies. This is the more problematic in institutional communication where all-important matters are at stake.

The same goes for members of underprivileged families who are all too often the clients of child welfare. They also often lack the cognitive skills to understand complex social procedures and have too few communicative skills to obtain the relevant information, explain their problems and reflect on their own contribution to these problems. The children of these families may very well have adequate communicative training to cope with their local world but still often lack adequate communicative capacity for negotiating complex institutions and for interacting with institutional representatives. As a result, they develop poor interactive agency, which makes them all the more vulnerable to the risks of modern society and may even destroy their interactive capacity to protect themselves against these risks.

The dilemma is this: protecting children completely prevents them from becoming complete, fulfilled members of society. Throughout life there is a fine, constantly shifting balance to be maintained between freedom and limitation; to do so successfully is crucial to the task of developing and maintaining the child's interactive agency. Such agency is necessary for children to live a relatively independent life. In the next chapter, I will look more closely at those structures of modern western societies that are important for the development of human agency.

FOUR

Social agency and social context

People are strange when you are a stranger.
Jim Morrison

People's agency depends not only on their personal history and interactional capacities, but also on the social context of their lives. Social agency is related to social identity and refers to what people have in common rather than how they differ (Verkuijten, 2005). A social identity is based on classifications, but although people may define others and themselves in relation to these categories, they are not completely determined by the class they are assigned to; they take an active stance and negotiate their identities. They may develop a sense of belonging to a social category that may confirm the social classification, but may also change that classification by transforming elements of the category. In his later works, Foucault (1985, 1986) analyses how people constitute themselves as ethical subjects through training and self-constitution and so try to resist the temptations of disciplinary society.

While most constructivist theorists agree that human agency is the outcome of social constructions, they differ in the degree of power they attribute to individual agency. In his study on the history of the prison system and in the first volume of his history of sexuality, Foucault (1979, 1980) argued that individuality, autonomy and citizenship are the outcome of disciplinary society. The ideal type of agent is western democracies is the autonomous person who can look after him- or herself without the help of others. But social categories are important conditions that help or hinder the realisation of autonomy, as they attribute different degrees of agency to individuals. Members of a highly rated social category will be attributed a high degree of agency, whereas socially deprived or disabled people are considered to have fewer social and personal means with which to govern their lives, a perception that serves to reinforce their dependency.

This chapter focuses on social structures that affect the development of agency. The dismantling of the traditions of western societies has brought about a radical transformation of social structures (Heelas et al, 1996). The decline of public authorities and the transformation of public policies have resulted in a different type of citizenship that emphasises autonomy, the ability to reflect on one's actions and entrepreneurship. The rise of the ideal of autonomy, as a developmental norm, is a major consequence of this transformation and is a central issue in this chapter. Although people in this new social order are considered to have full, free choice, whether they are actually able to achieve such freedom is questionable. The dominance of the 'free choice' discourse contributes to the illusion that people can fully rule their life. Traditional social structures may well have disappeared, but they have been replaced by new ones that actually limit the individual's freedom, even though they are paraded as freedom of choice. Some even speak of the 'pressure' of free choice.

These social changes have had a major influence on the development of children. In the first place, over the course of the past century the social and legal position of children has changed dramatically. Children and their parents are major consumers and, to a large extent, young people drive the information and communications technology market. In the second place, children stemming from families at risk often belong to specific social categories, such as minority ethnic communities, lower social classes and lone-parent families. Children belonging to such families often have fewer capacities at their disposal and fall behind in the race to make the most of their 'free' opportunities.

This chapter describes the fall of traditional society and the growth of local and temporary morals. A general neoliberal ideal of autonomy and freedom accompanies these 'new moralities'. The consequences of this social transformation for the development of children are illustrated by some recent changes in the legal rules of family life: the changed position of the judge in vice cases, the liberalisation of the Dutch Bill on choosing a family name and the growing significance of children's rights. These have all contributed to the reigning ideal of individual autonomy and the construction of new categories of deviance.

The dismantling of traditions and changes of power

Most children grow up in a context in which adults take responsibility for their upbringing. Yet this context has changed significantly over the course of history. The traditional family – formed by a heterosexual relationship solemnised by the Church (or a Register Office), leading to the procreation of children, with the mother staying at home and the father going out to work – is now just one arrangement among many others in which one or more adults (of the opposite or the same sex) take responsibility for bringing up one or more children, who may be foster and/or step-children. In most families, both parents work, both assume the role of caregivers and both have a substantial share in their children's upbringing. The stable, unchanging family that does not end in marital breakdown has become little more than an ideal for many (Smart and Neale, 1999), although people with children tend to have more permanent relationships and children may even prevent marriages from breaking up (Smart, 1997). Concomitantly, while children are now more independent of their parents, they appear to be more emotionally involved with them (Zelizer, 1994); at the same time, in public and semi-public spheres, children and adolescents are more strictly controlled than ever, for example, at school or when taking part in sporting or leisure activities.

These changes have led to different ideas about what constitutes good parenthood, which is part of a more fundamental shift in the mechanism of power in western societies in which relationships between adults and juveniles mirror the relationship between state and citizens. Before the rise of industrial states, the populace was governed by absolute monarchs and families by absolute patriarchs, with fathers having absolute power over all family members. This repressive type of power functioned well in traditional societies that were characterised by repetitive patterns of life and work. With the rise of the first free-trade cities, 'citizens' were able to resist despotic restrictions and to claim more freedom of movement. In these first civic societies, autocratic government was no longer feasible, for citizens were learning to take the initiative and make informed decisions for themselves. In many social areas, power began to function differently, exercising a reinforcing and optimising discipline rather than being merely repressive. In Foucault's (1980) account of these changes, people were invited, stimulated and encouraged to develop their skills, to cooperate with fellow citizens and to start new businesses, while, within the shadow of the ceremonial function of monarchs, a new disciplinary power could develop undisturbed. What was most significant about this new, modern form of discipline was the way in which it related to knowledge (of the subjects to be disciplined). Disciplinary power was 'an interrogation without end, an investigation that would be extended without limit to a meticulous and ever more analytical observation, a judgement that would at the same time be the constitution of a file that was never closed, the calculated leniency of a penalty that would be interlaced with the ruthless curiosity of an examination, a procedure that would be at the same time the permanent measure of a gap in relation to an inaccessible norm and the asymptotic movement that strives to meet in infinity' (Foucault, 1979, p 227).

Public policy became a system of disciplinary practices and strategies in the field of education, sexuality, child rearing and health. In family life, this led to the emancipation of women and children. A range of social agencies situated between central government and the private life of citizens penetrated social life in and around the family, with many aspects of private life becoming the targets of services and policies. The state adopted a detached attitude towards the family, content to facilitate whatever relational arrangements were found by family members to be most beneficial for themselves (van Nijnatten, 2000). But the possibility of legal intervention remained. In this psycho–judicial complex, the upbringing of children was regulated in a similar way to the Keynesian regulation of economic markets (Donzelot, 1979), parents having the private initiative to start a family with children and raising them according to their private beliefs, but within the margins set by the state. Paternal territory was progressively reduced and mundane family life was mainly supervised by mothers, while children were recognised as individuals with their own interests.

Since the latter half of the last century, the relationship between citizens and administration has changed radically. In the context of increased globalisation, the classical national institutions that were once key to the development of social identities have faded. People's sense of belonging to a culture or community through traditional social affiliations seems to have diminished. In addition, the ties between social experts and family members that were a characteristic of the welfare states of the 20th century seem to have loosened. Western European governments have decided that their administrations should operate at a greater distance from the private life of citizens. In the construction of their lives, people allegedly do not want to be hindered by general rules and professional advice; they would rather make their own decisions about their education and career, about their relationships and parenthood and about where and how they live, without being dictated to by social directives.

The dismantling of traditions has thus resulted in a radical change in the social position of the individual. People's daily experiences no longer correspond to custom and convention. In modern society, people are not expected to conform to fixed patterns of social relations or conventionally prescribed ways of life. Individualisation shows in the breakdown of the proletarian milieu, the introduction of negotiation in (family) life and the more flexible and decentralised organisation of work (Beck, 1992). Social relations have become mediated and dissociated from their (local) contexts, remaining reciprocal but no longer sharing a common locale (Thompson, 1995). The increased security of modern life has paradoxically led to a decrease in personalised trust (Giddens, 1995), while the unknown effects of some areas of new technology go, equally paradoxically, with greater ability to analyse data and produce statistical reports on all kinds of risk in other areas (Beck, 1992). People are more aware of the perils that threaten daily life.

Personal moralities and the undermining of the law

One indicator of the decline of previously accepted norms is the change in the (moral) position of judges in cases of offences against public decency involving juveniles. Throughout the 20th century, there was a decline in the moral interest of penal law in such cases, but concern has now reappeared in the form of public indignation at the blurring of certain moral standards. Now a multitude of isolated moralities rather than a single moral framework appears on the stage of legal action. In modern legal procedures, it is the victim who is of central importance and the role of the judge is reduced to one of mediating between parties, which means that the legal process risks becoming dominated by the personal emotions of the victim (Boutellier, 2002). A study of the changes in jurisdiction of vice cases between minors before and after the so-called sexual revolution, that is, between the periods 1963-65 and 1987-89 (van Nijnatten, 1997), demonstrates how the role of the judge has changed. Most cases from the earlier period would probably not have been taken to court in the later period. Exhibitionism, homosexuality and voluntary sexual intercourse between minors over the age of 16 would not have provoked a lawsuit in the later period, and very few prosecutions for vice led to child protection intervention during that time. In cases drawn from the later period, violence was the main reason for reporting a crime. In the earlier period, sexual morality had a repressive character and moral authority lay mainly in the hands of public authorities, while the role of parents was considered to be that of protecting the sexual morality of the family according to general public standards. In the Netherlands, in many cases the parish priest was a most important informant of the Child Protection Council. The judge was merely the last moral agent in the chain of authority. Family interventions at the cost of parental authority were most often taken on the basis of sexual moral considerations (van Nijnatten, 1988). An indecency offence was considered to be the very proof of a familial aberration.

Analysis of reports from the later period shows responsibility for sexuality being categorised as the individual responsibility of the juvenile concerned. In two thirds of cases (compared with the earlier period), the complaint was filed by the victim himself or herself. The parents' voices were only audible in the background. They testified that they rejected the notion of having strict control over their children, but expressed concern about the consequences of their children's behaviour. Adolescents were considered to be able to make judgements about their (sexual) relations without the help of others and to be sufficiently informed to be aware of the consequences of their sexual conduct. In sex education, sexuality was presented as a personal responsibility, and conduct worthy of legal intervention was presented both as a lack of personal responsibility and a lack of respect for fellow citizens. This, it seems, was what called for legal proceedings and court judgement, rather than any 'deviant' sexual preference. Thus had one general public sexual morality been replaced by another general norm, one in which individuals, as responsible citizens, negotiated and decided about the kinds of relationships they wanted to have. What was or was not considered acceptable behaviour was held to be an issue between partners rather than a public matter; only when one of the partners felt violated and reported a crime did the law begin to move into action.

The growth in sexual individualisation meant that judges had to give up their role as defenders of sexual morality. Judges no longer had a pact with the social institutions that brought vice cases to court, but assumed a passive role, only reacting when a victim reported a crime. That, of course, fits with the attitude that is increasingly expected from public institutions. The judge's task is to protect the space and integrity of individuals, not to limit citizens' freedom of choice. This was demonstrated in a recent Dutch case in which the juvenile court determined that rape is only deemed to have occurred when the victim has clearly stated that any sexual contact was against her or his will. The judges did not doubt that the sexual contact between a girl and six boys had been against her will, but because the girl did not clearly say this to her assailants, rape could not be proved. The girl said that she did not dare to say anything for fear that the boys would not let her go (*Metro*, 26 June, 2006).

The moral role of the court has diminished, certainly in the Dutch context. Nowadays, the task of the judge seems to be to mediate in local and separate conflicts between citizens rather than to defend a morality that is generally accepted in society. This is a good example of the individualisation of society. When each individual has his or her own morality, there is no shared concept of what is good (although there is a shared opinion about bad morality, which involves hurting other people), and accordingly the role of the court is reduced to settling conflicts between citizen. The dominant ideal seems to be that citizens should not be obstructed by public authorities in the exercise of their individual autonomy. They should have maximum freedom of individual choice and society seems to have the role of supporting individuals in achieving their personal life goals rather than creating a social order.

Personalisation and the illusion of unlimited freedom

'Freedom of choice', surely, is an ambiguous freedom because it is the exchange of collective control for the free market struggle rather than the emancipation of all individuals. A recent change in Dutch law giving parents the right to choose their children's family name illustrates this ambiguity. Instead of a child automatically receiving the father's surname, parents can now give their child either the mother's or the father's surname. Should the parents be unable to decide, the old procedure is invoked and the child receives the father's surname. Once chosen, the same family name will be given to all the children from that couple. The Bill has far-reaching consequences for children, but the rationale for the change in the law originated in public support for an equitable division of parental rights between men and women (with due regard for the children's interests).

From an emancipatory point of view, it is remarkable that the right to choose the surname of the child is reserved exclusively for parents and that children have no say in it. It is hard to understand why the state should be prohibited from playing any part in such matters and why parents should have this right. Would it not have been logical to give children the right to choose their own surname at the moment they reach the age of majority? Children's opinions on this issue are largely unknown, because nobody asks them. Cooper and Webb (1999) cite the case of a boy who, after living for some time with a foster family, stated that he wanted to stay with them but did not want to take their surname as his foster parents wished. The foster parents took this as a vote of no confidence and withdrew from foster care. Children appear to value continuity of care, but at the same time do not want to renounce their life history. It is evident that their name is closely tied with their existence and that it cannot be easily changed.

A more fundamental reason for not giving children or parents the full freedom to choose their family name is its function to connect the child to society. Liberalising the law on choosing a family name may convey the message that individual order is superior to the social order. Once the child thinks that he can manipulate the law, he is no longer inclined to submit to it, and less inclined to reconcile himself to the rules of society. It would then become more difficult to temper megalomaniac fantasies where the child imagines he can rule the world. The very moment that the child *subject*s himself to the social order, he becomes a *subject*. This is the confrontation with the unequivocal precedence of society. At the same time, it is the child's guarantee that parents cannot manipulate the law. So, quite apart from the justified claim of equal rights for men and women to be free to give their children their own surname, it is important that a procedure should be established in law. Perhaps the optimal solution to this conflict of warring individual rights is the Spanish custom of giving children the surnames of both parents and keeping that double name until they themselves marry.

The emancipation movements of the 1970s claimed freedom of choice from the Rousseauesque idea that there is no natural basis for male dominance over women, adults over children or state over citizens. The idea was to achieve justice by more equality and participation, but this, according to Foucault (1982), is just another way of becoming subject to a different regime of power. It is, however, indisputable that modern citizens have become less docile; they construct their own lives, claiming new lifestyles, moralities and relationships (Giddens, 1995).

Rather than simply reflecting a detachment of the individual from collective agencies, the individualisation process more fundamentally reflects a different relationship between self and other. More than ever before, people participate in organising their own lives at work, at school, with friends, in therapy. Individual choices are not free, as people often have no other choice than to choose, and their positions are still very much supported by social agencies: people often construct the multiplicities of their selves in contact with human services and their experts (Holstein and Gubrium, 2000). Individualisation is therefore not just a process of liberalisation, but also a transformation of dependencies and standardisation (Beck, 1992). Although people may seem to be in control of their own lives, they are dependent on fashion, market and policies. Individualisation does not only simply provide people with free choice but demands their active contribution as well. The growing number of options in the marketplace, whether for opportunities or commodities, demands skills and knowledge to make those choices in a well-considered way.

Not all opportunities are within reach of everybody and not all the choices that are made are well considered. The opportunity to organise one's life depends on a reliable self who is capable of assessing and attributing significance to the external events of daily life. The lack of such a 'natural' internal context may undermine autonomy. People differ in the extent to which they can trust such a psychological and social structure. Nevertheless, the ideal of the independent and self-contained individual, who controls his or her life and who has full freedom of choice and right of self-determination, has become the dominant ideal of personhood (Sampson, 1988). This atomistic vision, starting from the idea that human needs, skills and motivations develop separately from social interactions, puts emphasis on independence. It leads to a sharper contrast between successful people who are able to control their lives and those who lack such organising skills. In current society, citizens are supposed to be active and responsible people, who can look after themselves – autonomous citizens who have a flexible rather than a strong agency, can respond to changing situations and present aspects of his or her personality that fit into any social context.

The caricature of the self-contained individual is based on a unilateral idea of development. The atomistic view, which is the basis of the argument for equal rights, also provides theoretical legitimisation for egotism and rivalry. It leads to a reduction of the moral dimension, and to a social world in which people arrive at solutions on the basis of negotiated rights and claims rather than on the basis of principled deliberation. This ideology also neglects people's concrete, specific life conditions. It is easy to argue that one should remain aloof from the lives of one's fellow citizens when one knows little of the conditions under which they live (Tronto, 1993). This approach often ends in the formalisation and standardisation of relationships, as in contracts of care, which are separated from the specific features of people's lives and the specific needs that arise from them. Formalisation and standardisation make those relationships impersonal and interchangeable (Code, 1995), and provide no means for agents to understand the actual lives of their 'clients'. Care is divided up and allocated to specialised care agents in a manner that is more defined by their professional practice and convenience than by any specific needs of their clients.

To return to our case study, Jennifer has experienced this standard approach several times in her contacts with child welfare workers. To begin with, most of them approached her with a variation of this self-contained individual. In staff meetings, they discussed her dramatic history and were united by their concern about her future. When Jennifer was old enough to be invited to case conferences, they changed their discourse and tried to address Jennifer as a young woman on her way to adulthood. It was implied that soon she would be able to stand up for herself. It was confusing to Jennifer that she indeed had a claiming approach. Yet she was hardly able to negotiate, having little capacity to gear her desires and plans to the wishes and ideas of other people. Her claiming attitude is her strategy to organise external structures and to mask her uncertainty.

The isolated independent life is too easily presented as a universal principle of autonomy. It is considered to be in everybody's best interests not to be dependent on someone else. This is presented as an essential feature of human beings and implies that any non-autonomous person is an imperfect being: too little, too old, too slow, not smart enough. Naturally, not everybody complies with the ideal of the responsible citizen who is always articulate, the critical consumer who knows what is for sale, the finely balanced client who knows how to verbalise complaints and how to take well-considered decisions. Many people are not so active, critical or full of initiative. A person's capacity to take important decisions depends on the constraints of that person's life rather than merely the right cognitive competencies and relevant information. That is why attention to people's concrete situation and individual life history is an essential pre-condition of good help.

It is, however, possible to construe autonomy in a very different way and to take the alliance of people with each other as a starting point (Gilligan, 1982; Held, 1993). Solidarity and care may be more important than equality. Interventions that are undertaken out of concern for, and in the best interests of, the other may be viewed in a less negative light and do not have to be portrayed as paternalistic intrusion but rather as a sign of sympathy and respect. And in any case, paternalistic intervention may be justified by the argument that in the end it will lead to a socially responsible life. Autonomy flourishes once it is accepted that people are different from each other (Sennett, 2003). This is the common basis for accepting both each other's autonomy *and* dependency. Autonomy is only possible thanks to the mutual dependence of friendships, caring responsibilities and social activities. It would be better to speak of *relational autonomy*, referring to the possibility of functioning independently thanks to a network of relations. People have to be approachable. They also have to meet their relational obligations, based on trust, which are different from contractual obligations. There has to be an acknowledgement of the vulnerability of the one and the good intentions of the other (Sevenhuijsen, 1998).

For children of divorce, rather than the individual power of decision, a respect for autonomy should be allowed full play in the network of their relationships (Smart et al, 2001). It is the child's right to develop her own talents and prepare for a responsible life (United Nations Declaration of the Rights of the Child, article 29), which entails taking into account the interests and needs of others rather than just claiming her own rights. Such a responsible attitude is developed when the child is brought up by parents who are themselves able to balance their own and other people's interests. Relationships of inequality enable children to discover the proper use of power and, in the process, the human value of social responsibility in situations where the stronger person acts altruistically in the interests of the weaker. Parents who use their authority in the interests of their dependent children raise children who are likely, in turn, to be capable of doing the same with those who are dependent on them. The very nature of good parenting lies in treating children *not* as equals but in giving priority to their interests. Parents try to identify and meet the needs of their children rather than fulfil predetermined role obligations, and only in the last resort do they balance these with their own interests (Newberger, 1980).

The concept of relational autonomy fits with the new personalisation paradigm, emphasising both the need to gain control over one's individual life and the dependency on social structures. Free choice means having both different options and a socially responsible attitude. Becoming relationally autonomous includes both the liberation of external restrictions and the growth of internal discipline, or, in the words of Foucault (1986), 'care for the self'.

The claim for children's rights

The clamour for more children's rights is the logical result of the individualistic project. This claim was the main raison d'être of the children's rights movement, which in the 1970s and 1980s demanded equal freedom of rights for children. Some advocates argued that children should be eligible for the same rights as adults since they were full human beings; children should be construed as subjects and thus as right-holders rather than mere objects of concern and protection (Verhellen, 1998; Smart and Neale, 1999). As childhood is no longer 'an icon of stability among a welter of social flux and uncertainty' (Wyness, 1996, p 444), new legal arrangements are needed. By the mid-1980s, in various European countries, child legal centres were opened with the aim of informing children – and adults – about the legal position of minors and giving legal concrete legal assistance. The conceptualisation of autonomy, however, is crucial in this debate.

While it is true that most rights that protect adults' interests also protect those of children, the atomistic conception of the autonomous individual with full rights in society fails to take into account the developmental nature of the 'autonomy' of individuals. Basing children's rights on their assumed autonomy is tendentious, for, by definition, children are not yet autonomous, self-contained individuals. This is not just because they lack civil rights, but also because they are still naturally dependent; they are still insufficiently equipped, both cognitively and emotionally, to act independently in a reasonable way that could take into account both their own interests and rights and those of others. Children may therefore be said to have *additional* rights because they have special needs (Young, 1990); they have a right to protection, they have a special need of care and education. Before they can become autonomous individuals, children's education must begin from this strictly unequal individualism, and because of their insufficiency, their autonomy has to be limited by those who raise them (Baumrind, 1978).

More profoundly, the concept of autonomy is problematic because neither children nor parents live in an isolated world, but deal with common societal rules. They share a moral order on which children's rights and parental obligations are based. Children only come to belong to a society and achieve an autonomous position in it by abandoning their self-containment and living according to societal rules, accepting limits to their personal possibilities. To become individualised, the child has to socialise. A pedagogy based entirely on the right to self-determination could give children the illusion that the world is theirs to conquer as long as they stand on their rights and avoid too much involvement with other people.

In the protected area of childhood, children may experiment with social boundaries. If a child is not yet fully committed to legal obligations, she is free to experiment with social relations without being fully judged according to adult norms. Parents mitigate the consequences of their children's thoughtless actions and teach them what those consequences might be. Without this room to experiment, children would lose that vital opportunity to learn about social relations and to acquire their own positions vis-à-vis others. A consequence of this is that parents have the right and the obligation to think and act in the best interests of their children, as 'proto-competents', treated in a way that corresponds with their future status as an autonomous person (VanDeVeer, 1986). The limitation of freedom of choice is therefore often needed out of respect for the child's 'anticipatory autonomy rights' (Feinberg, 1980).

It is hard to draw an exact line between a mild, protective attitude that protects children from problems they cannot yet handle and an excessively protective attitude that keeps children from developing autonomy. Although children may show early cognitive independence in special social conditions such as divorce (Kogos and Snarey, 1995) or becoming a refugee (Wolff et al, 1995), this often results in serious emotional disturbances. This cognitive autonomy can hardly be taken as an adequate basis for granting children rights apart from an assessment of their emotional and psychological development (Helwig, 1993). Children benefit most from a mix of protection rights and autonomy, avoiding conflicts between the extreme positions of either totally denying a right to self-determination or granting free license (Hart, 1991).

In modern society, great demand is placed on individual personality and rapidly changing social conditions may be a source of fear for children with poor organising capacities. They are thrown on their own resources – an unfortunate situation for those who have to rely on external structures, because they have few psychological tools for introspection, reflection or self-detachment. The individualist model of basing child welfare on children's rights is therefore not necessarily in the best interests of all children. While some (the rich ones, the clever ones and the other lucky ones) may profit from legal support, many children from disadvantaged families would benefit much more from the implementation of a model based on parents' obligation to their children and public obligation to vulnerable citizens.

Autonomous entrepreneurs?

Children find themselves in ever-changing contexts – they move house and change schools and leisure activities, their parents get new jobs and their mothers in particular come under stress to combine work and childcare (Hochschild, 1989, 1997). Parental ambitions and household budgets are the main factors influencing strategic decisions about whether to send children to boarding school or pay other people to care for them, and are mainly the preserve of middle-class parents. Lower-class parents do not have the choice between work and childcare; they have to do both. Although men now participate in childcare more than they used to (Flouri, 2005), and although there is generally still a deep distrust of childcare outside the family, more and more Dutch parents nowadays choose professional daycare for their children.

Personal relationships nowadays are less anchored in the external conditions of social and economic life, and are held together by ties of romance and affection (Giddens, 1995). Parents feel a growing discrepancy between the new work ethic and the family values with which they were brought up (Sennett, 1998). The huge rise in the divorce rate can be seen as a breakthrough of the values of the world of work, flexibility, challenge and novelty into the world of relationships. The family has changed; while it was once seen as a natural phenomenon, it has become a variable context for intimate relationships that are not defined beforehand but rather arise from negotiation (Silva and Smart, 1999). And yet, although people now rely less on members of their family for support, they still consider them to be their most important safety net (Finch and Mason, 1993). Nor have the changes in the duration and basis of relationships resulted in different opinions about care and mutual obligations; children and divorced parents who no longer live in the same house still tend to fulfil their obligations to care for each other (Smart et al,

2001). Parents and children still construct continuity under conditions of radical changes. Modern relationships are reflective, partners permanently evaluating whether things fall short of expectations, their relationships tempered by these expectations. The social structures in which intimacy was previously organised are replaced by the involvement of self-confident people who take the risk that relationships built on romantic love may prove to be only temporary. The relationship is centred on intimacy, which calls for psychological involvement and mutual trust. The nature of family life, too, has altered; it has the character these days of individual projects of people who plan on staying together as long as it will be to their advantage.

Similarly, the relationship between adults and children has changed, with caregivers trying to find a balance between control and autonomy. The modern managerial parent governs by leaving as many decisions as possible to the child, encouraging the child's adaptive capacities and sensitivity to the needs of other people, and as a result enhancing the child's independence and self-confidence to act autonomously in different situations. In most families, pedagogical instruction has also changed radically. Many parents have an active policy of encouraging their children to use their abilities to live their lives and to solve their own problems. Their role is rather 'introducing' than 'stimulating' (Hallden, 1991). Children are seen as young entrepreneurs, and the owners of their lives, which makes them at least partly responsible for their self-advancement and care (compare Du Gay, 1999).

Confrontation with new and unknown situations, both at home and at school, seems to be a permanent feature in children's lives. In Dutch primary schools, children have to deal with a range of different teachers. As a result of a reduction in teachers' working hours so that they can spend extra time attending professional training courses, teachers no longer have sole responsibility for a particular class. Depending on the school's facilities, classes are divided into small groups that join other classes for individual tasks, or are run by another teacher. Although not all children deal with this type of change well, it is nonetheless considered to foster the kind of autonomy expected of small children.

Furthermore, learning with peers is one of the main goals of current Dutch education programmes. Very young children already learn in groups; they are asked to prepare their lessons together with other children from their class. When conflicts arise between children, teachers try to minimise their mediating role and encourage the children to resolve their differences among themselves. Such peer mediation appears to be successful (Johnson and Johnson, 1996). The pedagogue as instructor and counsellor has given way to the pedagogue as facilitator, the one who enables the child to exploit his or her talents and abilities.

Our modern, electronic world enables children to telecommunicate and get in touch with other people in a new way. They chat with their friends online and surf the internet for information. Teenagers in urban environments even organise their own safety online by constantly updating their friends about where they are going and what they are doing. The village is back in town. Despite these trends, it is still considered essential for good familial relationships that parents give their children plenty of attention, show empathy and spend quality time with them. The cult of individualism may have reduced the amount of time parents and children spend interacting with each other, but this does not mean that parents are distant or indifferent towards their children. They have ambitions for their children and explicit notions about what is good and bad for of their children's development.

Negotiation has assumed the role of the most important mode of communication between parents and children (DuBois-Reymond et al, 1990). Many parents set out their own (moral) position and – within wide margins – leave their children room to explore their own attitudes and to shape their development in their own way. Children are raised by their parents to all intents and purposes, but, at the same time, they are asked to assume an active and individual responsibility for their actual behaviour (Smeyers, 1992). Modern parental authority is ambiguous, because it is both the result of a determining structure and an appeal to take an individual, critical stance (Connolly, 1987). The 'demand to negotiate' enables children to learn the capacities they need to conduct their lives in a society that relies on the ability to adapt rapidly, to be critical of authority and to maintain one's balance in changing conditions rather than rely on experience and history. Rapidly changing life and family conditions also demand from the child the ability to manage many impressions in a short time.

Whether and how quickly children become autonomous depends on their life conditions. The extent to which children are bound by parental control may be determined to some degree by class. Children in middle-class families tend to have authoritative parents who combine parental control with negotiation and explanation, whereas children in lower-class families more often have authoritarian or permissive parents (Baumrind, 1968). Children from lower-class families tend to have fewer – if any – opportunities for the training in entrepreneurship, negotiation and acceptance of differences to which their middle-class peers routinely have access. As a result, a proportion may lose their way more easily and come up against difficulties sooner. These children and their families may therefore be also more at risk of being the subjects of child welfare intervention (Duncan and Brooks-Gunn, 2000). Children from middle-class families have learned from an early age to deal with child minders, teachers, coaches and so on, and may therefore be better trained for public life. For good reasons, parents want to help their children become good interactive agents by providing them with communicative skills. This enables them to find their way more easily in different social situations. Children with fewer social, cognitive and communicative capacities are less equipped to deal with sudden changes and more vulnerable to temptations that in the short run may seem attractive but in the long run often turn out to be against their interests.

Personalisation strategies do not overcome the unequal distribution of these features among classes and cultures in modern society (Campbell et al, 2007), as ownership of personal budget does not necessarily leads to a sound pattern of spending.

In personalisation policies, with their 'partnership' style of governing, children are involved more and more in decisions about their lives, both inside and outside the family. This, alongside claims for children's rights, has been one of the major shifts in the nature of adult–child relations. Although the capacity of children for self-realisation has become widely accepted, this change has not simply resulted in the emancipation of the younger generation; it has also been accompanied by a growing concern to control and regulate children's lives. According to Prout (2000), the late modern society's approach to children is ambiguous. On the one hand, children are seen as unfinished projects and objects of regulatory policy, which is evident in the field of education, where children are tested on more issues at a younger age and their lives described in terms of measurable 'competencies'. On the other hand, the emphasis is on self-realisation, inviting children to make choices on their own, involving them in relevant decisions and promoting a child-directed consumerism. In this very attention to self-realisation, inequalities become exacerbated, as economically or otherwise disadvantaged children have less facility to build their lives. This leads to positive discrimination in favour of those who can present themselves according to dominant mores and leads to the marginalisation of those who do not fit into the mainstream discourse (Shotter, 1993).

Traditional parent–child relationships are still common, but in many families they are more like friendships (van Wel, 1994). Children have a greater input into how their lives are shaped and more freedom to express their thoughts and feelings; they are consulted as individuals and have a say in their future. 'Identity' and 'negotiation' have become key words in planning and changing relationships (Giddens, 1992). But again, this is not a universal change and inequalities arise when some children do not develop this kind of capacity. Just as employees have to learn to be flexible and ready to adapt to a range of working practices in order to prove their value to their employer (Sennett, 1998), children have to acquire skills to move in rapid changing social contexts. Some authors even describe family processes in managerial terms: parents are 'partners in a common entrepreneurship' (Doornenbal, 1996) and time managers. Successful parenthood demands awareness of the effects of personal decisions; parents must cooperate and communicate in order to realise a common plan, taking each other's wishes into account. A new style of parental governance has developed, quite different from the previous top-down regime. Like the modern organisation, the challenge for the family is to combine interdependencies and (the need for) autonomy (van Nijnatten, 2000). Parental power is no longer a 'power over' but a 'power to', with parents seeking consensus rather than command. The success of this new enterprise depends on good communication and the ability to create a good atmosphere in the family. Like good managers, parents appreciate and encourage relationships, anticipate problems and try to prevent them. They wait for children to take initiatives themselves; they do not organise for, but with, the child. Their function is merely to provide protective and facilitatory frameworks. Like managers, parents now govern at a distance.

Despite this more democratic aspect of family life, children's lives are in other ways highly managed. Indeed, children grow up in this tension between freedom and restriction, between controlling strategies and an emphasis on self-actualisation. While parents try to commit their children to the family, at the same time they give them room to experiment with their growing independence. There is a fine balance between these competing demands and parents know that they will lose control if the scale is tipped too far in one direction. When they extend their children's freedom, they also increase their control over them because they are not convinced that their children have the capacities to deal with a complex and harsh society (Wyness, 1994).

Broken social agency

According to market ideology, welfare agencies have to present themselves as attractive to citizens in need – to their 'customers '. The principle of 'free' choice is considered to honour best the agency of service users (Le Grand, 2003). But it is the very ideal of life as a mainly individual and reflective project that produces drop-outs: single parents with young children who cannot combine the demands of a career with the affective needs of their children; people with poor organising skills; older people with fewer physical capacities; immigrants with poor command of the language. The neoliberal idea is that people can take care of themselves without any interference, whatever the context in which they have grown up and now live. Fellow citizens stay aloof, either out of indifference or from fear of being considered paternalistic.

Our case study Jennifer's chances of a warm welcome in (child) welfare are slim. She is an unattractive client, who hardly is able to speak about her inner world and explodes or becomes mute at the slightest provocation. She better stares out the window than getting involved in an incomprehensible discussion about care plans, relationships with parents or school. Jennifer is just not reflective enough.

The reflective self[1] is a typical modern western construction that flourishes in complex neoliberal societies with rapidly changing structures that make many demands on people; it is inhospitable to people who cannot, or can only inadequately, give structure to their lives. Many people who emigrate to western countries come from collectivist societies with formal, strict public administrations linked to strong social control. These people experience a cultural shock when they enter a society in which the public domain is little more than a collection of individuals; they soon find themselves judged condescendingly as incapable of living up to the standards of a modern and dynamic society. 'The gap between those with and those without the capacity to form their life is intensified when "choice" has become a widely distributed expectation' (Prout, 2000, p 307). The 'not so autonomous' individual has difficulty in combining different worlds, cannot anticipate new demands or take advantage of rapid changes and tends to panic, falling back on collective social agencies. These people will be classified in a less favourable way and characterised by the negatives of the autonomous agent: passive, non-organised, dependent, slow and inexpressive. Being a member of 'more at-risk' categories is considered a major problem. Special attention is paid to single teenage mothers, unemployed immigrant families and broken families with an addicted parent. When membership of a risk category is confirmed by actual behaviour, as so often happens in child welfare families, the categorisation of the families or individuals concerned becomes a definitive social identity. This social categorisation denies that the lack of agency of these groups is related to their material and social deprivation. Their poor capacity to be reflective and creative is based on their disadvantaged structural position.

A person's social identity is determined by membership of a particular community. Belonging to a problematic group is decisive for how that person is socially defined (juveniles who hang around, teenage single-parent families, child welfare families) and for whether they gain access to certain services. Belonging to one of these categories becomes a hindrance if it turns members of these groups into objects of suspicion; it provides a justification for monitoring them and enforcing social standards on them. Classifications may be differentiated further to provide a major tool for professionals – yet classifications stigmatise because they establish a negative social identity, regardless of personal histories. However, even negative categories may be significant for their members, because the sense of belonging to a category provides the members with a point of reference and an everyday structure to their lives.

The vast majority of child welfare families come from socially disadvantaged communities; bad housing, poor neighbourhoods and language deficiency contribute to their daily misery. Under these circumstances, it is much harder to live up to the standards of autonomous citizenship. The negative effects of contextual factors (such as poverty, maternal depression and poor professional support) on attachment patterns have been amply demonstrated (Peterson and Albers, 2001).

An additional hardship for socially disadvantaged families is the decrease in collective provision, which they need in order to structure their lives. In traditional society, feudal and clerical authorities governed relational life. The social positions of men and women, children and adults, upper and lower classes were clearly defined; the external locus of control was obvious. People with little individual capacity to organise their lives could rely on these social organisations to structure their world. In modern society, people are supposed to be entrepreneurial and provide for their own future income and health through private investments. Strategies are no longer directed at developing the social bonds between citizens (through national insurance based on solidarity) but at encouraging people to make their own arrangements for future. It is a policy that activates 'the self-promoting strivings of individuals themselves, in which each is to become an entrepreneur of his or her own life, running their life as a kind of enterprise for the advancement of themselves and their family, articulating their own demands for the protection and enhancement of their own "community"' (Rose, 1996b, p 322). But the freedom that goes with the ideal of entrepreneurship and non-intervention has different consequences for middle- and lower-class families. Middle-class people are better trained in self-discipline and better equipped to run their lives by cutting their coat according to their cloth. Most lower-class people do not live according to the ideal of the rational entrepreneur, an all-round individualist who finds his or her way around huge data files and enjoys an almost unlimited freedom of choice, who mixes easily with strangers and sees change as a challenge rather than a threat. Current society provides little locus of control and leaves much to the individual; therefore, people with little internal locus of control will have a tougher life and tend to lose out in the rat race of modern times.

From childhood onwards, members of marginalised communities get fewer social opportunities to develop a properly functional social perspective, despite social programmes that exist to help them. There are many social programmes that provide support for children; modern western states that ratified the United Nations Declaration of the Rights of the Child take children's rights as a starting point for family law and the organisation of child welfare. The risk of taking rights as a starting point, however, is that children may be condemned to minimal welfare. There are certain obligations owed to children that they can never claim for themselves. A good upbringing embodies ideals that exceed anything that could ever be claimed by means of protocols and rules. The belief that children can defend their own rights can actually inhibit adults from exercising their responsibilities toward them. Equal rights may well create the illusion of partnership, but at the same time mystify the social inequality that will still remain. Any drastic legalisation of relations in which children are involved would probably benefit only a small and intelligent minority, while destroying the social protection that shields the majority. The political credo of minimum intervention 'may be attractive to some, but in a world of basic structural inequalities, individual freedom can be so exercised as to undermine not only the liberty of others but also their human dignity' (Freeman, 1997, p 370).

Conclusion

The dismantling of society's traditions has resulted in a different configuration of social identity. In traditional societies, social identity was heteronomous and one's social status depended on the neighbourhood where you were born. In early modern societies, social identity was individuated and accomplished through personal efforts and capacities. In late modernity, it has become image-oriented, managed and strategically fitted 'into a community of "strangers", meeting their approval by creating the right impressions' (Coté and Levine, 2002, p 126). At the same time, the exercise of choice and judgement has become the dominant feature of human agency. It is based on the idea that people are able to recognise and pursue their life goals and that health and welfare services will compensate deficient agency and help people to express their goals and make their voices heard.

Modern society is an 'egocracy' (Verhaeghe, 1998); the individual is no longer freed from the group to start new relationships, but has withdrawn from almost every social tie. The 'struggle' to get one's accomplishments and abilities recognised as worthwhile for society (Honneth, 1995) has become harder. Group rules have been replaced by individual agreements. Much is permitted between citizens, as long as they agree. There is no longer a coherent or stable framework within which citizens make their demands on the administration and jurisdiction of society, and as a result these demands become increasingly paradoxical. In matters of their private life, citizens expect to be left at peace, but at the same time they demand stricter public policy in the case of the troublesome conduct of fellow citizens. They are negative about many legal procedures that only hamper their self-realisation, but at the same time want adequate legal recourse against fellow citizens who get in their way. This is not only an incoherent attitude, but also shows that moral involvement with the law is no longer grounded in common social standards. The moral force of penal law has been eroded, because although punishment may still fit the crime, it has scant bearing on the moral delinquency of the persons responsible for the crime (Boutellier, 2002). In the eyes of the modern citizen, the role of the judge is not to interfere in the private affairs of citizens, but to act within clear guidelines in so far as that citizen is obstructed by fellow citizens. The reaction of the judge seems now to depend largely on the preferences and the mood of the citizenry.

The relationship between the state and citizens has changed from one of patriarchy and total care to one of 'partnership'. Social institutions have withdrawn and in many cases only intervene at the request of individual citizens. This chapter has given some examples of this in Dutch society: in vice cases, the juvenile judge is no longer the active moralist but the passive judge who only reacts at the request of people who bring a case to court; which family name your children will receive has become a private matter and is no longer treated as an issue beyond the scope of the individuals concerned; and children's entitlements have become a central starting point for the organisation of the new Dutch family law. This is an example of the individualisation of children, who now have a direct relationship with the state and whose circumstances may be judged separately from their familial context.

The role of the state is further diminished when the child is treated as a partner who can rely on the help of the family court but is also held responsible for cooperating with the court. Child welfare may then cease being an institution that protects children's welfare, and instead become an agency offering its services to self-sufficient children when they ask for help. However, there is another aspect to these changes: although the centrality of children's rights may be seen as an example of empowerment, it may also be seen as a disciplinary strategy of self-government. Nor is it self-evident that children's rights give children a (stronger) voice. It is unlikely that many children will be able to participate fully in court proceedings or in the context of an imminent family intervention, in which case the advocacy of children's agency is no more than 'an inclusive policy that excludes' (Vandenbroeck and Bouverne-De-Bie, 2006, p 136).

It is an illusion to think that the advancement of individual autonomy is the only way to empower families and children. Nor is there good reason to believe that change in the ideological status of the individual represents the total withdrawal of state powers. As Foucault has so cogently argued, any power regime produces its own strategies and techniques of suppression. The relationship between citizens and the law has nowadays assumed features of the relationship between producer and consumer, the law and the judge producing what citizens ask or demand. As a result, one may be led to believe that the individual is superior to the social and even to life itself. This inevitably leads to disappointment when one discovers that it is not necessarily within one's power to have total control over one's life.

The previous chapters argued that limitation is a necessary condition for successful individual development. In a society that does so much to support the self-contained individual, it is remarkable that this essential precondition has been largely forgotten. Sometimes, individual growth seems to be the only remaining aspiration, with society reduced to serving this single aim. But the very erosion of the social hampers individual development because people owe their subjectivity and membership of society to the acknowledgement of their commonality.

Moreover, it the erosion of the social leads to asocial behaviour because people use their own interests rather than those of others as the guiding principle for their actions. Daly (1999) compares our condition with that of the dinosaurs that have been brought back to life in Jurassic Park and break out of their enclosure one night. We may think we are so modern that we can take any liberty we like, but then suddenly the monster in us breaks loose.

The emphasis on the self-contained parent and child means that free choice, negotiation and flexibility have become the central values of western society. It has also resulted in the marginalisation of those who cannot live up to these standards. Fragmentation, individualisation and cuts in welfare provision have eroded the quality of the provision of care for children and created a void between those who have the obligation to provide this care and those to whom care is due. It is this as much as anything else that places children's rights high on the agenda, since someone has to represent the interests of the children. In many situations, children appear to stand up for their rights better than might be expected, although in such cases they are usually defending basic living conditions. To achieve anything better, most children need the assistance of other people and of the state. Giving adult rights of freedom to minors will not automatically improve their social position. Child protection was created precisely for children who live in perilous conditions and who cannot stand up for their own rights and interests. The not-so-autonomous children will easily become the objects of social intervention, which is often dressed up as giving them back lost agency, but which in reality is further proof of their disempowerment. Recent developments would even seem to suggest that the ideal of autonomy is itself at risk as new welfare instruments reflect repressive ideas of living up to conventional norms of citizenship rather than disciplining citizens by way of self-investigation and self-government. We will return to this in the next chapter.

Note

[1] Holstein and Gubrium (2000) see human identity as a reflective accumulation that grows out of the different stories people tell, the accounts they give and the reflections they make on these accounts.

FIVE

Diagnosis and dialogue

Don't let the past remind us of what we are not now.
Crosby, Stills and Nash (Suite: Judy Blue Eye)

So far this book has analysed human agency at the level of individual development, social interaction and social structure. Although in reality there can be no such thing as perfect agency, and a stubborn wish to achieve such perfection could be construed as pathological, the desire to become autonomous is nevertheless considered a 'normal' attitude in western cultures. However, these cultures differ in what they consider to be the minimum level of agency that people should achieve. Consequently, different levels of agency between individuals may reflect different cultural backgrounds.

Parents help their children to develop agency. Children's developmental continuity is at risk when parents are unable to give meaningful context to the changes in their children's lives, that is, when they fail to instil in the child a growing sense of self-control and self-actualisation. When parents lose their grip on their lives, when they (think they) can no longer influence the course of their children's lives and find it difficult to develop a perspective on the future, this sense of discontinuity is likely to show in their children's behaviour. Parents face a series of ever-changing demands when bringing up children. All parents come up against problems and both expected and unexpected changes; discontinuity only occurs when parents are unable to construct a meaningful line through these events and to organise their life and the lives of their children accordingly.

In cases of discontinuity, the child's development is seriously at risk. This is when an assessment is needed to establish whether a (coercive) child welfare intervention is needed. Family court decisions resulting in restriction or abrogation of parental power reinforce discontinuity and confirm what most parents and children already know – that things cannot go on in the same way. The fact that public institutions get involved in cases of troubled parenthood means that child-rearing practices are considered to be matters of the common good rather than just private matters.

Child welfare assessment is not an exclusive intervention in a single incident, but serves the public goal of safeguarding and promoting social stability by distinguishing cases that need correction from cases that can left to sort themselves out on their own. Modern child welfare and the autonomous family go together, child welfare using as little force as possible to achieve social order while giving parents and children maximum freedom to live their lives according to their own beliefs: 'Governing people is not a way of forcing people to do what the governor wants; it is always a versatile equilibrium, with complementarity and conflicts between techniques which assure coercion and processes through which the self is constructed or modified by himself' (Foucault, cited in Lemke, 2001, p 204).

Child welfare is a people-processing institution (Prottas, 1979). It functions as an intermediary between the state and individual citizens, monitoring troubled families and preventing the development of more serious problems (for example, criminality or sexual abuse). Its goal is to preserve family autonomy by preventing unnecessary interventions without losing track of children at risk. This autonomy is not unrestricted, however; it is a disciplined freedom, for the project of child welfare is to produce normality by demonstrating deviance in troubled families (compare Foucault, 1979). Although child welfare interventions are often ineffective (in the sense that family problems cannot be overcome), their continued existence is not under dispute. First and foremost, the aim in child welfare is to help troubled families and children. In practice, however, any interventions are of limited value. The major effect of child welfare is the setting of standards of normality, by establishing the difference between troubled and untroubled families. In highlighting the divide between 'good' and 'bad' family life there is a disciplinary purpose underlying the monitoring of troubled families, and at the same time the hegemony of middle-class norms of rearing are reinforced.

Families are classified according to whether or not they are deemed to be in need of special attention. Categories of deviance are a major external tool for compelling people to live up to the standards of normality. In a small minority of cases, these categories are used to justify coercive interventions, but more frequently they put pressure on individuals to 'voluntarily' obey the rules and to live up to social conventions. This is not just a translation of external norms into internal values, but rather a complex interactional process in which general categories become embodied and enacted by people carrying out institutional practices (Mäkitalo, 2010). The actual meaning of categories of deviance only becomes visible in concrete interactions between people. They are tools employed to create a context and co-ordinate perspectives and activities of both institutional representatives and the clients of these institutions (Mäkitalo, 2003).

In this chapter, I will present a dialogical view of assessment. First, assessment is analysed as an interaction between a public institution and the private life of citizens. Second, assessment is considered in its historical perspective and in terms of the debate between advocates and opponents of a positivist assessment practice in child welfare. Finally, I look at the practice of the Dutch Child Protection Board, which has a monopoly in assessing family cases in Dutch family courts.

Child welfare intervention

Coercive family intervention usually comes into play when child pathologies are considered to be the result of serious parental dysfunction. As soon as it is evident that parents cannot raise or care for their children as they are supposed to do, a family court will abrogate parental authority and measures will be taken to guarantee the child's safety. As discussed in Chapter Four, family law in most western countries is becoming more and more oriented towards children's rights. This is not without risks, as interventions based on children's rights and without reference to the inadequacies of parenting may reinforce two mistaken ideas: that the child's right to be raised well is unrelated to the quality of parenting, and that parenting is dissociated from societal control. The very core of family intervention is the idea that the child's development is at risk precisely because of poor parenting. If family interventions were to be based exclusively on children's rights in order to avoid blaming the parents, this would be to commit these two profound mistakes. Children live under the protection of their parents, but within a framework defined by the state, which is more concerned with the moral standing of the parents than any actual risk to the child. Actual danger to the child is not in itself a reason for intervention. Children who are at serious risk will not attract child welfare intervention as long as their parents are doing everything a parent can be expected to do to avert the danger, no matter how ineffectually. A parent who takes his or her physically injured child to hospital need not necessarily have to confront a coercive family intervention. But if parents are addicted to hard drugs, a family intervention may follow even if their addiction has had no obvious effect on their children.

Giving children rights of self-determination in family issues is to give them oppositional rights, encouraging them to enter into legal conflict with those responsible for their upbringing. Children are likely to benefit more if conflicts are resolved in the intimacy of mutual dependency and trust, and by negotiation. The inquisitorial character of Dutch family law means that complex problems of child rearing are discussed in a family conference setting, where establishing proof means gathering as much relevant information as possible that may benefit the child in question (van Nijnatten et al, 2001). Using strictly legal procedures for establishing proof in family law cases would reduce complex disturbances in family patterns to their more obvious – and often more superficial – aspects, such as physical injuries that 'prove' (parental) abuse, because only these kinds of fact are accepted as evidence. Such an approach may fail to result in intervention in cases where children are really in need of protection but where no hard proof has been found. Conversely, it may lead to intervention that is based exclusively on hard legal proof but is insensitive to any positive aspects of the family situation. The children's rights debate needs to be backed up by an inclusive social policy that starts from the realisation of rights in the daily lives of children and their parents rather than one that implements children's rights from the top down.

Family court decisions are based on pedagogical norms. Coercive interventions are only legitimate in those situations where parental conduct, or parental failure to act, hampers the child's development of a minimum level of rationality, morality and authenticity (de Ruyter and Spiecker, 1993). In other words, child welfare interventions are justified when parents are unable to guarantee pedagogical continuity and to create or sustain intersubjectivity with their children such that the children are insufficiently equipped to organise their own lives and to develop a future perspective.

Current pedagogical norms correspond to the changed ideological context in which children are now raised. Nowadays, parents who raise their children too strictly and give them insufficient room to develop their own perspectives are criticised, whereas two generations ago such conduct would have been regarded as positive. At that time, parents would have been severely judged for exercising too little authority or for taking too liberal an approach towards their children (van Nijnatten, 1988; Komen, 1999). The standards by which families are judged have changed from the classical model of warm mother and strict father to an open, communicative parenthood in which parents negotiate and facilitate the child's autonomy.

Child welfare intervention is the legal confirmation of discontinuity within the family. In the case of young children, an official judgement of parental incapability is the justification for family intervention. Although family interventions are aimed at restoring continuity in the child's life, the whole chain of events, involving the child welfare agency, the court and home visits, disturbs the course of family life. Even though parents and minors are now more involved in decisions than they used to be, the core of the child welfare intervention is a devaluation of parenthood and a limitation of parental jurisdiction. The intervention will often have a radical effect on both parents' and children's ideas about the other and the self, which may result in anger and grief and lead to new discontinuities. The negative interpretation of the family's capabilities is reflected in other people's reactions ('that child welfare family', 'those antisocial parents') and may even lead to exclusion from social contacts and facilities and increased marginalisation. The ideas of child welfare families about themselves often do not accord with other people's ideas about them. Despite being weighed down by negative feelings of guilt, revenge, anger and despair, and despite being disqualified from parenthood, these parents still have (high) hopes about their future with their children.

Child welfare interventions demand an adjustment of parental identity; the more parents are attached to their parental roles, the harder it will be for them to assume another role. This adaptation process is inhibited if their future role remains uncertain for a long time, for instance when a family supervision order is renewed year after year without future plans being clarified, particularly concerning the child's future residence. Such an uncertain status may result in indolence, or may encourage the parents to become hostile, or to deny or minimise problems such as alcohol abuse (Forrester et al, 2008). This in turn only impedes their cooperation with the representatives of child welfare, who prefer the parents to reconcile themselves to the (negative) evaluation of their parenthood and adopt a passive attitude in the face of professional advice.

Professional expertise and client empowerment in child welfare

The societal role of child welfare has changed over time. To better understand child welfare assessment practice, we need to be aware of the different ways in which at-risk families have been considered; we need to look at the history of professionalisation and the role of child welfare expertise.

Before the Second World War, child welfare assessment in the Netherlands was authoritarian and dominated by family judges and court employees, who worked within a highly moralistic framework. The relationship between assessor and assessed was hierarchical, the child welfare employee looking down at the failures of troubled families. Family values, developmental conditions and quality of parenthood were judged on the basis of 'generally accepted' norms; the views of dignitaries counted more than those of family members.

In the 1950s, under the influence of American social work methods, a more therapeutic approach gained ground. Social work was presented as a profession in its own right, possessing expertise in human relations. The social worker knew how to deal with clients, how to help them regain a grip on their lives and draw on their reserves. This professionalisation resulted in the more frequent use of psychological and interpersonal models in the assessment of problematic family situations (van Nijnatten, 1988).

In the early 1970s in the Netherlands, residential workers protested against the child welfare establishment and against 'inhumane treatment' in child welfare institutions. Juveniles were still being locked up in isolation cells, welfare agents were taking decisions about children without listening to their views and juveniles were being stigmatised for the rest of their lives. The tutelary approach was said to *create* rather than to cure dependency, and institutions' inaccessibility had made them bastions of expertise rather than open professional communities. Clients were not allowed to read what was written and reported about them, nor did they receive a copy of such reports.

The protests in the 1970s marked the beginning of an emancipatory movement whose goal was to put an end to the subordination of clients. The starting point was to allow clients to verbalise their problems. In addition, child welfare workers tried to politicise their clients, making them more aware of their disadvantaged social position and encouraging them to see their problems as stemming from political and social, rather than individual, failings. Campaigners positioned themselves as equals rather than assuming a patronising role in relation to clients, although this often resulted in introducing new hierarchies. Another remarkable feature of this movement was that critical workers and clients used the law as an instrument to realise their goals, whereas previously the law had been seen as one of the cornerstones of the establishment. Indeed, it was once thought that emancipation might best be achieved by avoiding the law (Raes, 1996). As a result of these protests, the legal position of child welfare clients, parents in particular, improved significantly. Clients obtained the right to contra-expertise and institutions became compelled to formulate complaints procedures.

By the 1980s and 1990s, there was growing opposition to social provision as a strictly controlled 'market of welfare and happiness' (Achterhuis, 1980). The main planks of recent development had been the emancipation of clients and the embracing of legal procedures, but the result was a managerial approach to child welfare that put its trust in discipline, organisation and procedure (van Nijnatten, 2000). First, the costs of the (child) welfare state were considered to be too high, and the approach was still thought to be tutelary, therefore undermining the responsibilities of citizens (King, 1997). Second, it was alleged that welfare institutions were unproductive, bureaucratic and too distant. Changes in human relations, it was said, demanded a reconsideration of the top-down style of governing. Partnership strategies were introduced (Jessop, 1997).

Anxieties about the high costs of welfare were also related to a pessimistic assessment of the effects of social work methods (Stenson, 1993). Up until then, welfare services had been justified by reference to the client's needs, but this was now no longer considered to be sufficient. In order to be taken seriously, social work had to show the professional value of its methods and had to be made accountable. Social work, including child welfare, was called on to justify its activities by different yardsticks: procedural transparency, good 'assessment' methods, client participation, communicative (client-friendly) skills, quality management and audits. The new benchmarks of 'good governance' in child welfare were strict institutional planning (with computerised support), assessment of the quality of work by 'customers' and colleagues, and publication of output figures. Chapter Seven explores the effects of this new paradigm for the organisation of child welfare. Here discussion is limited to the effects on assessment practices in child welfare when the profession is asked to furnish 'hard' proof of its quality and effectiveness, and to introduce evidence-based assessment procedures.

Assessment: measurement or process

Researchers have often complained about the lack of any systematic evaluation of child welfare services (van der Laan, 2000; Loeber et al, 2001). They allege that new projects receive state subsidy merely by claiming to have new answers rather than by demonstrating their effectiveness. New, unproven methods, they allege, are too often accepted as the magic potion for child welfare, only to fade into the existing supply of services. These unproven methods tend to confirm institutional cultures rather than urge child welfare workers to reflect critically on their work (Sheldon, 1987). What is needed, according to this rigorous, hard-nosed school of thinking, is that child welfare workers should formulate 'concrete, testable goals in terms of developmental outcomes' (Slot et al, 2002, p 9) and build a body of knowledge based on evidence-based procedures, strategies and techniques (Sheldon, 1978, 1987; Sheppard, 1995); that is, the methodology of social science should be introduced, since this will enhance the possibilities of predicting the chances of success for particular interventions. According to this argument, the greater the body of empirically tested knowledge, the greater the chances of child welfare being successful. The underlying assumption behind this scientistic kind of thinking is that processes in child welfare services have a regular and general pattern, and that the role of science is to reveal them. The discovery of client characteristics, risk factors and family patterns should help prevent child welfare being no more than ideology in practice. This type of research looks for categories of human behaviour and explanations in terms of general and universal patterns. The value-neutral knowledge amassed will then be applicable in different kind of situations, apart from the client's and professional's interpretations. When this approach is accompanied by a database logic, the narrative character of the intervention is at risk. The procedure is then characterised by an additive, stacking causality rather than a linear one. The narrator as the one responsible for the construction of the narrative is replaced by the one who uses the database (Manovich, cited in Aas, 2005).

There is no doubt that professional child welfare should be open to critical reflection and that it could be improved by systematic evaluation. Yet evidence-based knowledge is only of indirect use in running human services. The process of clinical judgement cannot be reduced to the question of 'What works?'. Statistics and general patterns are only of marginal significance when it comes to individual cases in clinical practice; they are only relevant as far as they influence the professional's knowledge system. Biesta (2007) raises three objections to using the 'What works?' principle in educational practices. First, child welfare interventions are wrongly considered as just interventions or treatments, but rather are normative judgments about what is desirable in specific family contexts. Second, research can only present ideas of how to solve problems in an intelligent way rather than give us rules for action. Finally, the technical way in which research findings are forced on child welfare practices is a demonstration of a hierarchical view of the relationship between science and practice and is a threat to democracy itself.

The pursuit of evidence-based child welfare can even be dangerous when it leads to objectifying all kinds of elements in the life of clients – and in the relationship between professional and client – that are essentially subjective processes. That would be a form of reductionism that leads to a gentle dehumanisation of human situations and to misunderstandings about the tasks and functions of child welfare. Scientific involvement is only productive if essential processes and methods are contextualised and not objectified for the sake of control of the research design.

The methods and strategies of child welfare are not testable outside the context in which they are executed, otherwise they risk losing sight of the dynamics of human interactions. It may very well be an illusion that child welfare can be improved by a stricter control of its outcomes, because the structure of scientific testing is different from the reality of everyday child welfare practice. The application of objective 'measurement' to human subjects is to change them; it is a reflexive intervention that requires constant monitoring to see the effects of those changes as perceived by all the participants, not least the clients. Good evaluation studies are rare because the programmes examined and the social contexts in which they operate are complex and multifaceted.

A further problem arises if interventions and service programmes are investigated without a theoretical model; such evaluations easily lead to an enumeration of isolated measurements that at best are merely assembled in a matrix. In much evaluation research, it is unclear what has been measured, and allegedly demonstrated effects are often just presented rather than explained within any theoretical context (White and Stancombe, 2003). It is only possible to conduct a useful evaluation when it is undertaken in a clear frame of reference, in the context of a theory rather than a list of complaints, and with systematic reference to pathological insights, methods and the goal of the intervention. Service programmes are learning situations that are generated by the considered actions of individuals. Evaluation of service programmes should be based on 'the way that different subjects make choices in response to the range of opportunities offered in the course of a program' (Pawson and Tilley, 1997, p 38). The dynamics of child welfare services become intelligible when these processes of choice are taken seriously. In the everyday life of the client, a range of factors operates simultaneously, and these may best be investigated in the complexity of their interrelatedness. Child welfare is about parents and children having lost their agency, about child welfare workers trying to compensate for this loss through professional agency and by working towards restoration of family agency. It is simply impossible to disconnect clients and professional workers from the complexity of their relationship in order to study it (Taylor and White, 2000). Rather than asking 'What works?', we should be asking 'What can we do?' (Froggett, 2002). Such a question acknowledges child welfare's fallibility. The emphasis on best practice, benchmarking and the permanent focus on output and production is more likely to stimulate rivalry between agencies than support good care and cooperation.

The value of social science is in understanding what is going on in the lives of troubled families and in the helping processes rather than in proving the effectiveness of programmes. Scientific knowledge is one of the sources that child welfare workers can draw on. Besides scientific understanding, child welfare workers have at their disposal a wealth of cultural knowledge and professional ideas. The cognitive scripts that professionals use in their work contain both ideology and theory, and it would be impossible to work without them. Novice child welfare workers mostly rely on book learning; but the longer they work in practice the more they come to rely on their professional experience. During the first 10 years after finishing their studies, family doctors accumulate a great deal of knowledge from experience, which cannot be attributed to their formal education. Experience-based knowledge as well as evidence-based knowledge contributes to the performance of family doctors. They file this knowledge in 'illness scripts', which is a professional way of organising their memory. If these scripts are activated in the early stages of the diagnostic process, they contribute to 'superior diagnostic achievement' (Custers et al, 1996). They are necessary tools for structuring the mass of loose and detailed material of the client's case. The gist of child welfare – both in assessment and help – is to bring about changes in the daily reality of troubled families rather than to establish facts (which in penal cases is the task of the courts).

The transactional model in child welfare

There are currently two explanatory models that dominate child welfare research: the main cause model and the interaction model. The main cause model considers development to be the result of changes either in the environment *or* in the individual. It is a simple model that presupposes that individual shifts may be attributed to internal or external forces. The interaction model is a variant of the main cause model and distinguishes the child and the environment as different factors. In this model, the child's development is explained by a set of factors that accomplish certain effects in connection with each other. This interactional paradigm shows up in balance models and schemes of protective and risk factors (for instance, Rutter, 1987; Willemse et al, 2003). Studies based on this model have produced relevant information for child welfare workers and contribute to professional standards. The question, however, is whether they are of help in clinical practice; are they useful tools to help understand clients' conduct or which professional reactions are appropriate to bring about the desired changes?

Predictions, in the sense of how a certain effect may be anticipated under certain conditions, may be useful in epidemiologic studies, but are too general to comprehend relations in the complex biographies of child welfare families. The more formal the concepts, the less they are likely to match people's idiosyncrasies and the less they may contribute to a better understanding of the thinking and actions of child welfare clients. The more complex the social phenomenon, the harder it is to find the term that describes it. The notion that families can be mapped by assembling facts is illusory. Rather than aiming at a complete representation of the 'absolute' truth, we should pay attention to the various interpretetations op the people involved. Their interpretation of what is true is most relevant (Holland, 2004). Child welfare is social work about relationships between people who are trying to make sense of their lives. Therefore, assessment can hardly be considered in isolation from treatment; the exchange of meanings during the diagnostic process put things in motion.

A major problem of causal and interactional approaches is that the client is objectified as a carrier of features, symptoms and problems. The professional is positioned as the expert and the one with the responsibility to diagnose, while the client is ignorant – a black box to be opened by the professional. It is the task of the professional to honour the client's autobiographical expertise and to relinquish his or her position of superior professional knowledge. Hermans and Hermans-Jansen (1995) emphasise the diagnostic and therapeutic process as a meeting of two different kinds of expertise. Peräkylä (2002) shows that these types of expertise do not clash as clients use counter-arguments on different domains than professionals, and are cautious, leaving the professional evidence 'intact' rather than questioning it.

The transactional model gives in to the main objections of the causal and interactional models, and acknowledges the client's contribution to any meaningful interaction in care. This would seem to be a much more appropriate way to study the processes between child welfare workers and troubled families. The transactional model starts from the idea that various factors in the child and in the environment interfere with each other. Changes in the client's situation influence the client's behaviour in as much as they create the conditions that determine which changes are possible and which are impossible. The client's response to the new situation will further change the nature of the situation in a way that cannot be predicted beforehand, because no one knows at the outset how the client will actually react. In the transactional paradigm, effects cannot be attributed exclusively either to the client or the professional. Child welfare workers and clients are both sense-making individuals. In their mutual relationship, they process information from their own perspective and reintroduce this as new information in the framework of the interaction. Concepts are explained, repeated, put into a different perspective and constantly changed.

Child welfare is very much concerned with the production of meaning, with both partners contributing to new meanings through their interaction. That is why the essentials of the dynamics between professionals and clients can never be fully externalised and split into isolated parts to be studied separately. Each observable fact is a part of a larger, meaning-bearing whole. Clients evaluate their relationships with child welfare workers; that is, these relationships have a moral and subjective nature rather than being merely an instantiation of general patterns (Jordan, 1978; Parton, 2000). Child welfare workers proceed clinically – by listening to the client's story, investing energy in the reconstruction of narratives in which clients present themselves as helpless and victim, and seeking for opportunities to generate new meanings together with the client. The quality of an assessment grows as client and professional together reach a realistic description of the problematic situation, a description that also contains a new perspective on the future (compare Jordan, 1987). According to a transactional view, the workers succeed better by referring to the concrete opportunities offered by the client's actual situation rather than pre-established categories. The direction of the changes can hardly be forecast and depends both on unforeseen circumstances and the moral positions taken by client and professional. Hence, child welfare has an informal nature, whose proper aim should be changing perspectives rather than the applying solution strategies and serving up standards recipes.

Diagnosis is a complex interpersonal process in which interpersonal relationships, cultural expectations, professional wisdom and chance all play a role. It is often a moment of great uncertainty in the client's life, which is already characterised by a surplus of doubt and insecurity. It makes little sense to try to reduce the client's uncertainty by presenting models, calculations and scientistic predictions, even if clients want that kind of certainty. It would certainly preserve the illusion that life can be controlled, but what many clients do not realise is that this external knowledge only creates new dependencies (Parton, 2000) with hidden manipulative tendencies. It is the child welfare worker's task to unmask those underlying manipulative structures and to help the client to live a life with all its uncertainties. External standards are necessary but are insufficient to simply remove the uncertainties in relation to the client. It may be better for the child welfare worker to take this uncertainty as a starting point and approach the mutual relationship with the same hesitation as the client (Miehls and Moffatt, 2000).

Moreover, it is relevant for the professional to empower the client to gain maximum control of the communication. This is shown in the extract below of an interaction in one of three diagnostic sessions in a youth psychiatric department of a hospital. The therapist's intention is to map the emotions and motivations of a young boy of nine. The therapist (T) is aware that talking about his inner world may be problematic and has proposed that the boy (S) also work on a magic puzzle cube.

1. S: 'Well, I did not come so far yet.'

2. T: [Smiling] 'Hmm.'

3. [Pause 7.09–7.13 (minutes)]

4. S: 'This is good … then t– still differently.

5. [Pause 7.18 –7.30]

6. T: 'You are very patient, aren't you?'

7. S: [Smiles] 'Hmm, hmm.'

8. T: 'Are you such a patient man at home, as well?'

9. S: [Shakes his head smiling and looks at therapist] 'Huh, no!'

10. T: [Laughing] 'Huh, no? Ha ha ha…. How come that you do manage here to be very patient?'

11. S: [Keeps occupied with the puzzle and looks at her. Shrugs his shoulders a little bit] 'Don't know.'

12. [Pause 7.45–7.59 P plays with the puzzle]

13. S: [Looks at T] 'Can it also become a rectangle?'

14. T: 'No it has to go in there [takes the casing] … it was in there, with one layer out of it.'

15. S: [Takes casing] 'Oookaaay, then I might as well make it in here.'

16. [Pause 8.10–8.21 P plays with the puzzle]

17. T: 'In between I would just ask you if you want to give some marks.'

This extract shows that the boy uses his puzzle work to control the dialogue about his inner world with the therapist. The boy shows his pride about his puzzle performance (1) and the therapist reacts positively, followed by an explicit compliment about his work (6). She formulates this compliment as a question, inviting the boy to talk more about his patience. The boy does not pursue the question, and then the therapist asks if he acts at home in the same way as in the therapy room. Now the boy looks up, showing that he is triggered by that question, and denies, at the same time expressing that he had to think hard about that question (9). The therapist makes light of this by laughing and concentrates her next question on his positive performance in the therapy room. The boy has no answer and concentrates on his puzzle, changing the framework of the interaction from a discussion about his inner world to talk about the puzzle. The therapist follows this change, and answers his question. After a long pause, the therapist tries again to return to the therapeutic framework and asks him to award points for affects, which she records. Both client and therapist use the framework of playing with a puzzle to make light of the onerous task of discussing cognition and emotions about the self. The boy uses his involvement in the puzzle as an instrument to organise communication with the therapist and so manages to have the situation well in hand.

The child welfare worker's task is to make a sufficient contribution to enable clients to solve their problems and to help them give new meaning to their lives. It is the professionals personalities, not just their skills and techniques, that is crucial in achieving these goals; control of the self is what distinguishes the successful professional child welfare worker. Any negative reactions from the client should be contained (Winnicott, 1965) rather than parried; uncertainties are not allayed by trying to convince the client that the future will be problem-free or that any problem may be solved by professional expertise. That would imply that the client's contribution is irrelevant, whereas the goal should be to support the client in regaining control.

Good assessment is possible if all aspects of the family's problems are openly displayed. There is no single correct conclusion and any conclusion is only tentative. Constructive child welfare starts from the idea that the chances of effecting change are enhanced when clients have a realistic view of what changes are feasible and when they have to reconcile themselves to the forces beyond their control. The challenge is to find a middle way between unrealistic expectations and the nihilistic attitude that they cannot do anything about their lives. Child welfare is often criticised for not formulating its goals and strategies. This may be true, but this criticism is also the sign of a naive optimism that life can be controlled by the unbiased description of a problem and, accordingly, an absolute strategy to deal with it. Detailed enumerations of facts from the client's life, descriptions framed in behavioural terms and tests using external objective standards are no guarantee of a good understanding of the client's problems. If standardised child welfare were possible without reflection and without dialogue, it would be more efficient to leave the work to bureaucrats and clerks who could execute their standard procedures. The sad thing is that the amount of bureaucracy in child welfare is an indication of the belief in just such a standardised procedure. The features of troubled families, the biographical past and future of children and their parents, and the professional's ideas and knowledge are not disparate elements, but all function in a meaningful conversational dynamic between professional and family. It might be better to look for an *acceptable* plan rather than for the ultimate plan (compare Holland, 2004).

Child Protection Board

Decisions to intervene in families are usually arrived at after years of voluntary assistance, during which time clients and professionals have come to realise that action is needed to safeguard the continuity of care for children. In the Netherlands, decisions to restrict or abrogate parental power are taken on the basis of Child Protection Board inquiries. The board is a department of the Dutch Ministry of Justice and presents petitions to the juvenile court for judgements regarding the custody or guardianship of children, and international adoption. The board presents petitions concerning legal propositions for custody, suspension of the execution of custody, provisional guardianship, and dispossession and restriction of custody. These petitions are based on an investigation of the social conditions of the child and the family. An investigation is only begun when there are indications that children are seriously at risk and parents cannot fulfil their responsibilities. There are then several interviews with family members and information is collected from people who are professionally involved with the family.

'Discontinuity' was defined earlier as a disturbance of parental practice, an arrest in the process of the continued production of meaning and a rigidifying of familial roles that influence the child's development in a negative way. It was also explained that discontinuities are of a narrative nature: the inability to control the course of life with the use of words (symbols), to develop a perspective on life, and to project a future description or image of the self as a person who can take parental responsibilities. Various discontinuous family situations may lead to child welfare intervention: for example, when a mother can no longer keep her family in order; when a father resorts to physically abusing a crying baby because the noise irritates him; or when a juvenile no longer trusts his or her parents, and, after repeated outbursts of anger, starts acting out. In all these situations, acceptable standards of care are eroded and children are at risk. Social workers from the Child Protection Board then try to find out why this has happened.

In the normal course of events, the Child Protection Board's report confirms the familial discontinuity, resulting in an intervention that puts an end to the unacceptable behaviour. Yet the board's assessment may also be considered to be the beginning of the process to reinstate continuity. The report may contain ideas on how parents can regain responsibility and obviate further need for intervention by child welfare services. The inquiry may also set goals for improvement based on an assessment of clients' problematic past. Child welfare intervention may lead to the reinstatement of parental care, but there is no guarantee that the problems will be solved in the end. If no improvement is achieved, children may not return to their parents and may be cared for by others.

There are areas in which scientific rigour may be relevant to child welfare – the taxonomy of scientific research methods, for example (Sheldon, 1978). The formulation of working goals and the description of strategies and desired outcomes may improve systematic work in child welfare, as long as they do not become a template that kills all creativity. The assessment of child welfare may be compared with the empirical cycle in scientific methodology, in which theories, hypotheses, reflection and evaluation are at the centre of the investigatory process. An essential aspect of the critical approach in scientific methodology is actively to seek evidence that will refute a hypothesis. The scientific method of advancing knowledge by the Popperian (1959) logic of falsifying hypotheses is not feasible in the context of social work. However, a softer approach that clearly owes a debt to scientific methodology is the 'cyclical' working model: problem description, plan of change, evaluation, revision of problem description (including the conclusion that problems have been solved if that is the case) and so on. This method makes it harder for the professional to hide inaccuracies behind a curtain of technicalities and jargon and certainly serves to promote reflection. The Dutch Child Protection Board uses such an empirical cyclical model in assessment procedures. Ideas about the nature of family troubles are made explicit in working hypotheses and tested. The model comprises six phases. The board starts by formulating a provisional assessment question about the nature of the family problems. In the second phase, a working relationship is founded and areas of special attention are explored. In the third phase, the assessment question is confirmed, hypotheses are formulated and a plan of inquiry drawn up (which is discussed and agreed by a multidisciplinary team). In the fourth phase, the hypotheses are tested. This may lead to an answer to the assessment question in phase five, and a subsequent multidisciplinary consultation and decision. The assessment is then reported.

Working with an empirical cycle in child welfare assessment leads to fuller description of results in the relevant fields of investigation, especially in those categories covering the child's development and their personal characteristics. The child is given a more central place in the investigation. Moreover, the investigations are better founded and multidisciplinary expertise is more often used to describe and explain the developmental conditions of the child. As a result, there is less chance that relevant factors are overlooked (van Nijnatten et al, 2004).

A criticism of this model, however, is the technocratic approach used by child welfare workers in 'sorting and prioritising information and using this to optimise practice to its best effect' (Webb, 2001) without including the elements of the social context that make decisions in real life so complex. Although the cyclical model encourages reflection and the concrete realisation of ideas, there is always a risk that relevant differences in opinion about the nature of the problems are buried by the formulation of the hypothesis. If child welfare worker and family do not arrive at a uniform formulation about the nature of the problems, it may be better to let these differences serve as the start of a new attempt to gain common ground. An excessively rigid adherence to the cyclical model may leave too little room for the unpredictable nature of the client's future; it can lead to devaluation of the agencies of child welfare worker and client in their mutual dialogue. It is important that the Child Protection Board worker should make the clients aware that the professional's view of the family problems is only one perspective and that it will be subject to negotiation before it is worked out in a final hypothesis.

There is a wide gap between the advocates and opponents of introducing social research methodology into social work. Parton (2000) sees this as the gulf between different conceptions of social work, on the one hand as a rational technical activity, and on the other as a moral practice. This distinction should not be drawn too sharply, however. It should not imply that social workers acting as moral practitioners perform irrationally or lack professional expertise. I agree with Parton that the introduction of empirical methodology into social work does tend to reduce the complex, contingent and conflicting reality of clients; it does not solve the dilemmas that social workers have to deal with in their practice. Overriding emphasis on output, on formal procedures and production may simplify procedures for managers but does not lead to an effective answer to the problems of clients. Moreover, the new assessment forms that have been introduced in many child welfare agencies reflect state policy goals rather than help professionals to record sound information. The use of these forms tends to produce a non-narrative approach that seeks to confirm standard questions in the forms rather than the client's story and leads to a 'descriptive tyranny' (White et al, 2008). This is a step backward from the disciplinary approach in which the goal is to collect personal stories and to stimulate self-investigation. For child welfare agencies formulating their mission in terms of 'empowering' clients, a non-narrative policy is likely to be problematic because it undermines rather than supports the client's agency.

It is an illusion, therefore, to think that scientific methods of evaluation will lead to objective knowledge that can then be used as a 'reliable' instrument in child welfare. Nor does the impossibility of attaining objective, verifiable knowledge mean that child welfare is merely an amateurish line of work based on impressions and subjective experience. It is perfectly possible for child welfare to be a professionally organised activity, which means working with well-approved methods and well-considered techniques; but what is of the essence is that it must accept, rather than exclude, uncertainty.

Conclusion

There is strong tendency to assess people on the basis of the premise that a person's traits (for example, intelligence) can be measured in the abstract, unrelated to the context in which the individual develops and functions. Yet individual behaviour is always mediated action against a cultural background that contributes to the individual's performances. Agency occurs at three levels: personal development, interaction and social structure. At each level, agency develops as a result of contextual factors. At the level of personal development, the influence of primary caregivers is crucial. Infants need a stable environment to develop a solid self-image, which involves caregivers showing an unconditional positive regard. If such a steady context is not provided, the child may develop serious mental disorders. In the most serious cases, this may lead to a loss of a sense of reality, and, during sudden and unexpected events, a retreat into delusion. Once the child has constructed a more or less solid self-image, she needs a conditional rather than an unconditional parental approach. The child now has to acknowledge the rules of society and learn to live within its limited capacities. Parents help to establish these limits and gradually disillusion the child; otherwise the child will have difficulty in dealing with the limits that social life imposes.

The development of interactive agency takes place through the dialogue between the child and people in its direct environment. In the process of looking for common ground, children will understand the world according to their parents. If a child lacks basic trust and fails to accept its difference from others, she will adopt a hesitant and passive stance in interaction with other people. The child will be unsure whether her perception of the world is shared by those she loves. Children who are uncertain whether their interpretations are acknowledged or commonly shared will have difficulty in make their voice audible; they will have problems in constructing intersubjectivity, and lose their communicative ability to organise their world.

In the main, child welfare interventions are the last act in the drama of family discontinuities. The investigations of the Child Protection Board and the decisions of the family court are the confirmation of such discontinuity. At the same time, the starting point for child welfare workers to restore continuity has to be the psychological reality of the family members. Pathologies in human agency have a dialogical nature; the child's development depends on the continuity and responsiveness of others, while their social position depends on the extent of their involvement in the social process. It is well known that members of marginalised communities participate less in social processes.

Because the nature of family problems is mostly dialogical, the solution to these problems also has to be found in the communicative practices of these families. What parents and children need is effective help in seeking for and expressing new meanings that will help to organise their lives rather than learning new competencies. Such help is about rediscovering the words to structure their experiences in a way that allows each of them to be someone who can change while also remaining the same person. The child welfare worker can help children and their parents to find the words to develop new perspectives and so rebuild continuity in their lives. Future transfers and changes may then be couched in words that are meaningful for themselves and for others.

Assessment is an interactive and contextual process; both client and professional contribute to the meeting and try to come to an agreed account of the nature of the family problems. Science may contribute significantly to an improvement in the diagnostic process, but can never be implemented as such in daily clinical practice. General patterns of developmental factors, for instance, are an important source for the assessor, but they do not offer an adequate set of instruments to answer the question of whether parents can raise their children adequately or whether a (coercive) intervention is the right decision.

In a constructivist view of child welfare, assessment is first and foremost a process of reflection rather than the execution of previously acquired knowledge. It is the attempt to achieve a common and comprehensible framework with which both client and worker can identify. Making an assessment is starting the recovery process, a process of interpretation, negotiation and attunement. In the assessment, the future perspectives of the family are scrutinised. This is an open future, not a prescribed course that can be calculated on the basis of statistical data. Indeed, the uncertainty of the diagnostic process should be seen as strength rather than a weakness. Assessment involves acknowledgement of the client's and the professional's distrusts, doubts and disbeliefs; it is the study of how clients cope with difficulties from the past and uncertainty about their future. Child welfare workers try to support parents and children to live with the ambiguities that are part and parcel of life. Certainly, if assessment were centrally concerned with the problem of raising children, a transactional perspective would seem the best theoretical basis for reflection on the dynamic relationship between parents and children. In this perspective, parents and children are seen as active agents engaged in making sense of their lives rather than merely the unfortunate victims of internal or external forces, and as moral subjects with some choice in how to live a good life (that will enrich the other) (compare Sullivan and McCarthy, 2004). The most important element is that assessment should not be a professional judgement followed by an effort to coerce the family member into acceptance of that judgement. Rather, it is a search for the clients' own accounts, for their own understanding of their problems as a starting point for further considerations. Hence, it is an ongoing process of understanding the client, a process that never reaches a terminus (Anderson and Goolishian, 1992).

Triumphalist views of the effect of evidence-based child welfare are naive. They are based on the idea that any problem within troubled families may be solved as soon as enough sound ('objective') knowledge is obtained regarding complex social and psychological phenomena such as motivation, memory, exclusion, legal procedures and institutional communication. In such a view, the potential of social science is overestimated. Child welfare cannot be reduced to the exercise of certain skills in complex daily situations in which people become stuck in one way or the other. Nor can clients be considered as vacant subjects waiting to be supplied with good advice and life skills. It is highly unlikely that there will ever be models capable of fully comprehending the complex interactive processes between people. Indeed, a strictly positivistic approach may actually cause harm, in so far as these programmes take the complexity of the client's problems, unexpected turns and creative solutions, or the helper's idiosyncrasies, to be nuisances that prevent us from knowing which factors lead to which effects.

Of course, science has its contribution to make to a systematic procedure in the assessment of child welfare. Nevertheless, the impossibility of achieving objectivity should be acknowledged and critical intersubjectivity accepted as a serious alternative in which inquirers permanently and actively seek debate with colleagues with different points of view.

SIX

Change and co-construction

Love is hard to believe, ask any lover. Life is hard to believe, ask
any scientist. God is hard to believe, ask any believer. What is your
problem with hard to believe?
Yann Martel

In previous chapters, the dialogical nature of human agency has been discussed
on three different levels: individual development, social interaction and social
structure. Children may display pathologies at any level: when their development
is interrupted or slows down, when they are unable to make their voices heard
in conversation with other people or to live on the margins of society, or when
they are not brought up according to accepted social norms. Various social
programmes exist to support children who display symptoms of dysfunctional
agency: orthopsychiatric services, courses in social communicative competencies,
and compensation and participation programmes.

Child welfare agents operate mainly at the interactional level. They often have to
deal with clients who have poor interactive agency as a result of a severe personality
disorder or because they live in marginalised communities. Problems of individual
and social agency soon become manifest in encounters between professional and
client. Personal history and social status combine to affect the way parents and
children talk to child welfare agents, making institutional communication between
professionals and clients difficult. In addition, the scope for interaction between
professionals and clients is constrained by external societal and economic forces.
This means that the impact of any intervention is limited at both the individual
and the social level. A client's experiences cannot be undone or changed in the
course of a brief intervention and a few conversations about that person's past.

This chapter discusses the restorative actions of child welfare, mainly at the level
of interaction between children, welfare professionals and families. Child welfare
agents aim not just to provide services to clients but also to 'deep personalise'
(Leadbeater, 2003) – to help clients become self-organising and the designers of
their own lives.

Dialogical child welfare

Child welfare intervention is often initiated by juveniles or parents who get
in touch with a child welfare agency because they want help for one or more
family-related difficulties. If this kind of help does not work out well, or if for
any reason the problems become so serious that the child is seriously at risk,

further family intervention may be based on a court order. This kind of legal involvement throws family life into turmoil.

As difficult as child rearing may be, most parents regard it as their natural domain. They start a family with the idea that it will bring them happiness and that they will be able to guarantee their children good and safe lives. Child welfare intervention changes all this. When a court order limits or abrogates parental authority, the social consequences are huge: in their own eyes and in the eyes of others, parents have failed to raise their children properly, the children's loyalty is put to the test, and in many cases there is little chance that the parents will regain control of their children's upbringing. It is therefore no wonder then that many parents oppose child welfare intervention; it makes them feel rejected and humiliated and they imagine that the world is conspiring against them and that they have been cut out of the decision-making process. Even if some parents see child welfare intervention not as a limitation of parental authority but rather as a change for the better, they may still feel distressed by the fact that they have put their child in this position, ashamed about the disruption caused to the family and unfairly judged by other people.

Clients' narratives often disclose how they feel trapped by their situation and see no possibility of a change for the better. Clients are frequently the prisoners of their own destructive stories; they picture themselves as defenceless victims of an unfair and uncaring bureaucracy. They tend to have a rather unrealistic view of their own contribution to their problems, and yet at the same time see intervention as proof of their personal failure. For this reason, they have little self-confidence in their dealings with public services and tend not to do themselves justice in their interactions with them.

Child welfare cannot provide the certainties that families wish for. Indeed, uncertainty and ambiguity are at the heart of social services (Parton, 1998). Child welfare has no foolproof solutions to all family problems. In the transactional mode, child welfare tries to restore some kind of continuity in interrupted lives, to help families regain a grip on their lives to help clients take a more detached view of their situation. The intention is to improve the child's situation by getting the parents to reflect on their parental position. Is reflective language strong enough to overcome their resistance to change? The discussion below is first and foremost about the potential of dialogical help, the effort to help children and their parents tackle their problems through the work of narrative reconstruction.

As with anything that concerns children's upbringing, child welfare should ideally have a constructive and communicative character. Even in cases of coercive family intervention, most child welfare workers will seek the client's active participation. The client's responsibility is to follow through – on a permanent basis – with any changes in their lives that are suggested as result of the intervention. This is only possible where the will to change exists. Dialogue is crucial, because that is where meanings are exchanged. Yet the scope of changes that can be achieved through communication is limited; communication may encourage clients to try to alter behavioural patterns that have become entrenched or change their social situation, but personalities and societies are not so easily changed.

Clients' difficulties are the result of individual problems in the context of a particular set of social and economic circumstances. Child welfare interventions therefore take into account both personal and environmental factors in the client's situation, and tries to bring the two together. This, of course, is not solely a matter of helping individuals adapt to their environment but also of changing the social conditions that contribute to individual dysfunctional behaviour. Child welfare traces the roots of problems in neighbourhoods, in family situations and in the child's or parent's individual history. The aim is to enhance parents' abilities to take care of their children and to help them be more active in their upbringing. This may mean helping parents to discipline their children better, or helping them find better accommodation or providing information about day care. It may also mean that the child welfare agent, when reviewing the family's affairs, concludes that something must fundamentally change if further harm is to be prevented. The aim is always to help parents to help themselves, to develop new prospects for the future or to simply deal better a reality that is difficult to alter.

Narratives

The stories child welfare clients tell reveal the difficulties they experience in their lives. They often lack the narratives that provide people with a sense of coherence and continuity in their lives and feel that they lack the capacity to belong and to behave according to social norms. However, just as good parenting involves giving children individual autonomy by limiting their freedom, when the law requires child welfare parents to be distanced from their previous child–rearing methods the potential for the parents to gain insight into their lives is created. By reflecting on their lives, and composing and telling new stories with the help of a child welfare agent, these parents – and their children – may be able to recover a sense of continuity and stability. Of course, not every narrative works in this way for everybody. The stories told may remain incoherent for the individual and for others, or they may be fantasies that make things out to be better than they really are. Words and narratives do not necessarily express the truth; rather, they are provisional accounts of what the narrator experiences as reality.

Communication is the most important instrument child welfare workers have at their disposal in their efforts to change the attitudes and behaviours of families at risk. The goal of dialogical child welfare is to help families to reconstruct their lives. The encounter between professional and client (and this may be the parent, the child or both parent and child) may result in an exchange of meanings, perhaps with the client relating how his or her life has taken its course without them having any opportunity to influence its direction. In this scenario, the client's poor ability to organise his or her life has already become manifest in the narrative. The child welfare worker's role is to react to the story by showing understanding, proffering professional experiences and introducing alternative interpretations, but also by asking for biographical information and the client's considered opinion. Standpoints may appear for the first time; the professional or the client may repeat the other's phrases as a first step towards a shared personal formulation. Professional and client may also give different interpretations of what has been said by the other. Hence, two separate construction lines exist in parallel, the first containing information and interpretations that are adopted by the client, and the second line including personal and new interpretations by the professional (Elbers, 1992). At a symbolic level, new conceptual links become possible, involving new interpretations that make new experiences possible. Dialogical help thus supports the client's process of construction and reconstruction rather than reporting an objective reality that has no link with the client's own perceptions. Dialogical help is not an attempt to explain to clients what is going on in their lives, nor does it give them the tools with which they can change their lives fundamentally. That would presuppose an objective reality that is both knowable and manageable, and clients who can give direction to their lives in a thoroughly rational way (Lovlie, 1992).

People's future takes its meaning from the goals they set for themselves, but the most important aspect of this is the process of symbolising: formulating and reformulating rather than reproducing the precise content of what is formulated (MacIntyre, 1981; Anderson, 2002). Narratives are of central importance in dialogical approaches, for they help people to find new words to describe their images and to look at the future in a different way. Those reformulations help them to alter their perspective and regain a grip on their lives.

Dialogue helps clients to realise that the 'reality' of their life is to a large extent a constructed narrative plot with openings for different versions, rather than something that is fixed and futile. It helps them to consider their circumstances as *more or less* the result of chance, contingent rather than absolute, and yet still their reality. This may make it easier to relinquish an all too fatalistic view of life. The aim is not to find the ultimate explanation of a situation or a solution for all the family's problems, or place these problems in the context of some absolute 'truth' about families, but rather to negotiate and construct an account of life that can be explored and developed. Narrative child welfare is a non-controlling approach to explanation that leaves room for what we not (yet) understand. What we do not know and what we will never know must be accepted as a part of the human condition rather than regarded as suspect. The client is confronted with accomplished facts but is assured that there is no one optimal way to interpret and to cope with them. Life looks different when you approach it from a different angle; it may become bearable again when the author is back at the helm of his or her life narrative. In the line with Vygotsky's theory, interventions may be more effective when professionals co-construct new parenting practices with their clients (for example, getting clients to put their children to bed, share family meals, and do chores with their children such as washing up dishes) and then accompany these actions by reflective words that highlight the child's needs and conduct.

In child welfare meetings, clients are helped to reorganise their life by giving new (shared) meanings to it. The client may learn to overcome barriers that could not previously be overcome; for example, a mother who frequently gets into trouble with municipal social services because of her fits of temper may learn to control herself and negotiate with the authorities in a socially acceptable way. Changes may also entail a growing awareness on the part of the parents that they will never wholly regain parental responsibility. Even then, it is the child welfare agent's task to convince the parents that their role is not over and that they, as parents, can still have a major and positive influence on their child's life. This will only be possible, however, if the parents' own feelings of disappointment, loss, inadequacy, anger and shame, to name but a few, are acknowledged by the professional during their meetings. By always returning to the same theme, the child welfare agent tries to help the client create alternative views on the reality of their situation. Change is considered to be an interactive process, with the professional creating a relational and secure context in which the client feels supported. In this interpersonal interaction, the client's situation is discussed, debated and re-described until the client succeeds in building up a new narrative account of their situation that becomes part of the way they perceive themselves. Child welfare workers look for common ground with the client and look for suitable ways to help clients articulate and change perspectives on their family situation; in other words, they help the client to find their own words.

Dialogical help is aimed at dismantling troublesome patterns that may have become habitual in the lives of clients. On an interpersonal level, during meetings between professionals and clients, new interpretations of the client's situation emerge and are repeated until they become established in the client's inner speech (Vygotsky, 1978). The higher mental functions of people who react in an uninhibited or unsophisticated way to life events are often underdeveloped. Social services professionals may best support such clients by helping them to develop the meta-cognitive skills that enable them to reflect on his or her emotions and change unwanted routines of conduct (Miltenburg and Singer, 1999).

An open dialogue is the most successful way of gathering various different views on the family situation and encouraging a process of self-examination (Hermans and Hermans-Jansen, 1995). Seikkula (2002) developed a dialogical method in a treatment programme for psychotic patients and their family networks. It is a requisite feature of the programme that the client attends the professional discussions of his circumstances, but as a silent observer. In the course of the meetings, the therapist aims to show an understanding of the client by reformulating what the client has previously disclosed; space is created for the client and his network. Professional colleagues are then asked to give their views on the client's situation, rather than to advise or determine with certain techniques how the client should see his life and organise it. An open dialogue with psychotic patients and their network results in the empowerment of the client's conversational position; in Seikkula's method, clients succeeded in expressing themselves in symbolic terms and relying less on anecdotal ways of speaking

(Seikkula, 2005). In other therapeutic settings, a non-directive and withholding approach also enables clients to express themselves in a more sophisticated and unreserved way (Muntigl and Zabala, 2008).

The idea of dialogical help is that a coherent life narrative, in which a line of continuity is constructed, is a change for the better. Personal persistence is critical for developing agency. In narrative-oriented cultures, more emphasis is put on the changes in the personality, whereas in western mainstream cultures, the immutable character of personhood is more usually stressed in the process of developing individual agency (Lalonde and Chandler, 2004). But there is no single ideal way for people to recover from a painful past. Failure, deviation and regression belong to the struggle; there are no standard success stories. Breakdowns too may play an important role in the life of clients (Harvey et al, 2000). The primary aim of dialogical support is to make clients the authors of their life stories, helping them to name and contain their problems, and then search for stories that locate the cause of the problems outside themselves (White and Epston, 1990). Together with the client, the professional analyses the consequences of the problem, separating the problem from its effects, and distinguishing between those effects that are unavoidable and those that may be prevented and what role the client may play in preventing them. Such a strategy can help the client overcome feelings of impotence and indifference.

By distancing themselves from their problematic situation clients are able to tell a different story in which they are no longer the victim but take a more active position and gain control of their lives. They themselves, rather than their problems, become the agents in their lives (White and Epston, 1990). One particularly helpful strategy in this process is to get the client to look for moments in the past when he or she did find solutions and made good choices. This helps the client to develop a more positive self-image. If the client can tell these stories more than once, the narrative gains a more solid basis and provides coherence and an experience of continuity between past and future. In the mediated approach (Bauer and Bonnano, 2001), clients are encouraged to reconsider the meanings they attributed to past activities (before any traumatic events that may have triggered their current problems) and to use these again in the present. The idea is then to internalise these meanings. The aim of this kind of intervention is not to restructure the client's entire past. On the contrary, events from the past may restrict a client's ability to master his or her life, because the memory of traumatic events where the client was unable to come up with adequate answers can serve to reinforce feelings of weakness. Rather, intervention is aimed at emphasising the client's strengths as well as limitations. The goal of the professional is to help the client develop an overarching position in relation to his or her situation, and a sense of detachment from it.

The moral nature of social services

Dialogical help is reflective, assisting clients by enabling them to step back from their personal experiences and to develop the self-awareness that allows them to 'look' at themselves from a distance. The professional may support the client in this process of self-reflection (compare Guidano, 1995). The client who previously attributed their problems to external, intractable circumstances may now look at them as real and concrete issues that can be dealt with. Change may be achieved by training the client to be more self-reflective, to compare her routine responses with alternative ones, and to create new, meaningful ways of approaching situations. The professional's function is to create the conditions for the client to change, but it is not in his power to control when and how the clients will realise this change. Controlling clients' actions would reinforce their former experiences of passivity, weakness and incapacity, and would only lead to false adjustments. The crucial thing is that clients should feel encouraged to find their own words to describe their experiences and to formulate new life perspectives. The function of the professional is to endorse the clients' accounts, not to realise these accounts on their behalf.

When care professionals are able to listen well to their clients and, rather than corroborate the client's existing emotional understanding, give them the confidence to believe they can make a difference to their situation, they create the conditions for change. This is the moment when the personal and the social become interconnected. Dialogical help assists clients to accept the limitations of their situation and to become strong agents by recognising the imperfect nature of life. As soon as clients acknowledge these limitations, they can distance themselves from the idea that they are the victims of an invisible and abstract system of injustice.

Professionals cannot prescribe how life should best be lived in an objective manner; it is not about clients learning the perfect way of life according to any preconceived ideas or achieving a good score on a personality test. On the contrary, child welfare is concerned with what constitutes a good family life in the eyes of parents and children, according to the society in which they live. There is never a single, definitive answer to such a question; uncertainty and ambiguity will always be at the heart of it (Guidano, 1995). The trouble is that many politicians and managers in child welfare prefer a rational–technical model that promises a simple, objective standard that can be controlled. Such an approach, however, is deeply flawed, because it negates the essential aspects of the construction and negotiation of meaning and symbolisation that are essential to human social life; valuable information would be lost in such a quest for objectivity. Child welfare is a transactional process in which the client's actions and reactions help to determine the further course of the intervention; the professional's actions and client's reactions mutually affect each other. Isolating, formalising and atomising the events in troubled families only serve to distort these families. The complexity of their situation is better dealt with by recognising the practical-moral nature of the problems.

The claim that rationality and technique are the keys to optimal child welfare leads all too easily to paternalism. The assumption that the child welfare agent has a monopoly on wisdom makes any contribution from the client superfluous. If the proper route to good family life has already been laid out in a scientifically certified script, what would be the point of asking parents and children to recover their autonomy? This would be no more than an illusion. Rationality and technique are necessary preconditions for engaging in professional actions. The good child welfare professional is fully informed of the methods and strategies that can be used and have been effective in other situations. Moreover, the professional draws the client's attention to the improved chances afforded by a more detached approach to the problem, and points out the different positions the family members occupy in relation to others. Integration of these various positions helps to (re)construct continuity. Above all, child welfare professionals should encourage clients to become agents, to take an active role in conversation by articulating feelings, perspectives and possibilities for change.

Dialogical help does not just encourage clients to replace their destructive narratives with new stories in which they play active roles, but also highlights their moral and social obligations. Professional help encourages clients to reflect on their own positions within society. It helps them to take on reponsibilities and to relate to political principles and moral ideals (Rose, 1996a). It is an encouragement to restructure and take responsibility for one's life. The active role of the client is crucial; the client's acknowledgment that there is an alternative to an existing situation is the first step towards concrete change. This vital recognition is what care professionals must support.

Co-construction and empowerment

In the dialogical approach, the idea is that the client contributes to the development of new stories and that this helps them to better understand the nature of their problems. The relationship between professional and client is not a hierarchical one of the expert and the ignoramus. Both are architects of a project of co-construction, the development of a shared interpretation of the family situation. The client's version is not necessarily the whole story, but the client has a major role to play in the common effort to understand the nature of the problems. This principle of co-construction is played out through family conferences, which start with a meeting between the client, the client's family network and professionals, all giving their view on the family problems. After an initial assessment of the outcome of the meeting, members of the social network gather in a confidential meeting and draw up a plan to deal with the family's problems. They then bring their plan to the professionals and negotiate over the help they want to receive. The aim of family conferences is to ensure a more active role for the client, the family and close contacts, and to encourage co-operation and exchange of knowledge on an equal basis. The idea is that there is a certain amount of power and knowledge within the family network that does not exist within the professional and legal systems (Doolan, 1990; Turnell, 2010).

External events such as family conferences may be a turning point in the way reality is conceptualised, enabling clients to see their situation from a different point of view. The client is then able to question what was previously accepted as normal; experiences are interpreted differently in another frame (Goffman, 1974). In a dialogical relationship, the client is the agent with biographical expertise and the child welfare worker is the agent with professional knowledge and clinical experience. Both types of expertise are combined to feed the reconstruction of the client's views and evaluation of his situation. The client draws from a huge stock of personal memories that are not available to the professional, but these biographical issues assume a new meaning in the context of the relationship with the professional. The professional can assess whether her expertise is useful in a particular case: the main thing is to recognise the client's input and to tailor his response accordingly. Once there is more information about the support available and what part is expected of the client, there is a much greater chance of client and professional coming together with the same sense of purpose. Shared knowledge and decision making are only possible when the client's role is recognised. To map clients' views of their situation, Hermans and Hermans-Jansen (1995) developed the 'self-confrontation' method, in which clients are encouraged to relate significant events and reflect on past situations, thus creating a historical overview of different 'I' positions. This helps them to construct a coherent narrative based on memories, reflections on the present, and positive and negative expectations about the future. This method is only likely to be effective when the client is willing to participate in active self-investigation, rather than being merely curious about the outcome of a test or leaving the responsibility to deal with his or her problems to the professional. The professional invites the client to tell his story and provides support if the conversation flags. The final goal is that the client should formulate a conclusion. If there is something lacking, or there are lapses or contradictions in what the client says, the professional invites the client to retell the story.

It may be a slow, difficult process for many clients to arrive at a different view of their lives, but it is the only way for them to regain control. A solution-focused strategy may help to engage clients' powers rather than dwelling on their problems and poor strategies to deal with them. This approach has proven to be effective in coercive care, especially when clients are given the opportunity to verbalise their current situation (de Shazer, 1991; de Jong and Berg, 2001). Clients are invited to assume authority for what they want to change and how this can be done. The client's expertise is supported by the professional taking an 'unknowing position' (Anderson and Goolishian, 1992), asking the client to talk about their experiences and outlook. The client is encouraged to come forward with a more or less new version of his life history. He is invited to explain what his world is *like* rather than being asked merely to repeat what he did in the past and to justify his way of life to others. The solution-focused strategy is a common effort to generate new meanings on the basis of the autobiographical issues raised by the client. When people tell their story, they present their past to the professional, whose own input comprises general knowledge and professional expertise that is a closed book to the client. The dialogical effort to reach a common narrative understanding makes child welfare a constructive process in which, little by little, clients reformulate their life story differently. The power of this approach may in the end be more in the process of negotiating, tuning activities to one another and *coming* to an agreement than in the arrangement itself (cf. Shotter, 1993). Understanding is a never-ending, dynamic process that usually develops slowly by negotiating and testing presuppositions. Even though reaching shared understanding is difficult, the mere process of trying to achieve common ground literally *moves* people. Narrative child welfare is not about establishing any one version of the client's past as the correct one, but rather using fragments from the past as a moral-practical source that can help the client to live a life that he or she thinks is a good life.

If the client succeeds in becoming the author of his or her own story, family situations previously given up as hopeless may be revisited. If the child welfare professional avoids merely relying on former assessments and other professional evaluations and instead allows the client to participate in the dialogical process, she will be going against the grain of most interventions. This will surprise parents, especially in situations involving mandated care. Child welfare clients are in general accustomed to other people telling them how to live their lives, what is missing in the way they manage things and how they should do better. Although a child welfare intervention is always a shocking and far-reaching event in families, it need not necessarily have a negative impact for the rest of their lives. Even if a child does not live at the family home, there are still opportunities for improving the relationship between parents and child. It is relevant here that the child welfare professional should pay attention to past events that have worked out well and that demonstrate the client's strength and perseverance (McMillen, 1999).

Interventions turn the households of child welfare families upside down, but they are also moments when a new meaningful horizon may become visible. It would be naive to suppose that dialogical help is the panacea for all families at risk. Discontinuities in child welfare families often persist despite years of intervention by social services. It is frequently the case that no help is sufficient to solve a family's problems. Poor organising capacities are often passed on from generation to generation when the lack of adequate mental and psychological continuity is exacerbated by poverty, poor schooling or social isolation. Sometimes family tensions build up to such a pitch, or have become so deeply entrenched, that child welfare intervention is insufficient to reinstate continuity within the family. In these cases, the child welfare involvement will assume a more permanent character and parental authority will not be restored. When families evince little hope of any change for the better, child welfare assumes responsibility for safe developmental conditions for the children. But even in situations of little hope, nothing is ever permanently fixed, as has been demonstrated in open dialogues with schizophrenic patients (Seikkula, 2002). The task of child welfare agencies is to look constantly for the clients' agency, to search for possibilities to reopen the dialogue with them in the hope of involving them once more in relevant aspects of their lives. Rather than presenting herself as the expert who has the answers to all questions of life, the expert assumes the role of the analyst who queries practices, supports symbolisation and takes notice of irregularities in people's accounts (Arnaud and Vanheule, 2006).

A dialogical strategy falls short of helping our case study client Jennifer on her way to adulthood. Her foster parents were persistent in pursuing this course of action, but time and again had to face up the fact that it was beyond the bounds of Jennifer's possibilities. It was one of the main reasons why she could not continue to live with the foster family. Co-constructions and changes of perspective were too overwhelming for Jennifer. She experienced this kind of language as threatening and withdrew whenever a discussion was started. Yet the continual availability of the foster parents appeared to be an important external structure for her. Surprisingly, she developed a new linguistic strategy with her foster parents. Discussions at a distance appeared to be a possibility. Telephone calls could be announced by text message or not answered and sometimes led to a useful exchange of information.

The child welfare professional

Constructive and narrative approaches in child welfare are different from the rational-technical approaches that have come to dominate the field. In the current technocratic orthodoxy, professionals are seen as connecting with clients through modules in social contracts. This approach is inadequate because it does not have sufficient relevance to the (re)construction of meaning, which should be at the heart of human social services. If the client's problems are not central to the relationship between client and child welfare worker, the problems will simply recur. A client who expects the child welfare worker to have the solution to all his problems, and either makes himself totally dependent on the professional or rejects her altogether, cannot be helped by professional advice. It is not just a question of the client lacking information; he will also lack initiative and confidence in his own competencies. The professional must give the client some idea of what to expect: what the child welfare worker can or cannot do, the limitations on her time, and so on. This more cautious approach also protects the professional, who would otherwise run the risk of believing that she can solve all the client's problems. Child welfare workers who think they have the solutions for their clients' problems and who demand total commitment from themselves often suffer burn-out. They are not only setting unattainable goals, but also labour under the illusion that they have a monopoly on wisdom and solutions (Vanheule and Verhaeghe, 2004). No child welfare agent has the solution to every problem, and no child welfare agency can meet all the needs that clients present to it. The value of child welfare is in humanising problems that cannot be properly understood by the client alone, rather than in making up for what the client lacks. The essential feature of welfare provided to the people who seek the service's help 'is permeated by a quality of care that shows that they are being treated as one human being in difficulty and distress would wish to be treated by another' (Butler and Drakeford, 2005, p 650).

The more serious a family's problems, the greater the need for constant and encompassing care. Parents or children who cannot organise their lives and have to exert ever greater efforts to experience any kind of continuity are wholly dependent on the quality of their environment, in the same way that young children are totally dependent on their parents in the first years of their life. These clients benefit from constant structuring of their external world: clear arrangements, rules and tasks. Improvisation or sudden changes can wreak havoc and generate insecurity, and often result in clients becoming aggressive towards themselves or others. They are dependent on the willingness of others to take responsibility for them. The care they need is concerned with creating a protective, structured environment. Child welfare plays an important role here in a practical, organisational capacity.

For parents and children who find themselves overcome by problems, child welfare provides more immediate help. Clients who become overwhelmed by their problems find themselves unable to take any decisive course of action in their lives. The problems become all-consuming and they find it difficult to adopt any position of their own. In this case, the child welfare worker's role in relation to the client is similar to that of a parent's in relation to a child – to strengthen the client's agency by setting boundaries and challenging him or her to take up a position.

The task of the child welfare worker is not to be a therapist but to help the client to become independent by building up individual and interactive agency. This entails encouraging family members' capacity for reflection, to get them to take up a position in relation to their situation and to create space between themselves and the problem. Members of troubled families often feel totally dominated by their problems and incapable of changing anything about their situation. They have not the slightest notion of how to assume a position and do not see their difficulties as real facts of life. Reflection may help them to free themselves from this oppressive situation.

How is 'reflection' defined here? It means showing clients how feelings of insecurity and oppression can be entertained at the level of the imagination, the aim being that they might eventually gain insight into their own circumstances through being able to distinguish between factors that are personal and those that are structural. Child welfare workers also demonstrate that such feelings are common, recognisable human emotions that other people have in comparable situations. The reflective nature of child welfare meta-communication is especially relevant in the interactions between child welfare agents and family members.

It is a continuous process of achieving mutual understanding and checking to ensure. that each other's intentions have been correctly interpreted. The role of the child welfare worker is to help clients to find the words to express what is going on in their lives. This demands an open attitude on the part of the worker, to allow the client space to investigate inner affects ; it is not an opportunity for the worker to project her professional expertise or her own interpretation of the client's situation. It may be tempting for the worker to resort to her professional know-how because it articulates dominance over the client and may function as a defence against professional anxiety over the uncertain and ambiguous character of child welfare service. However, a dialogical approach aimed at supporting the client's agency requires the professional to tolerate ambivalent situations where it is necessary to wait and see if the client can find a solution. The professional has to take care not to dominate the situation when it is not strictly necessary.

Transforming family positions

Parents tend to be highly sensitive about any conversations that take may place with professionals in the context of a child welfare intervention. In these cases, their child-rearing practices have been discredited by the court and they are uncertain about the role they may be allowed to play in the future upbringing of their children. They often feel that they have failed in the eyes of the world. For this reason, social workers involved in childcare and child protection work endeavour to ensure in their dealings with the family that the parents do not suffer further loss of face. In addition, parents will try to present themselves in as favourable a light as possible in these circumstances and in most cases the social worker will corroborate any such representation. For the social worker, however, there will always be a tension between involvement and the need to maintain a degree of independence. On the one hand, he needs to become involved by placing himself in the position of the parents in order to see the problem from the family's point of view; on the other hand, he has to remain independent and safeguard a safe environment for the child. In child welfare, the dilemma generated by the conflicting demands of care and control becomes very apparent and manifests itself in discussions between agents and troubled families (Grossen and Apothéloz, 1998; van Nijnatten, 2006a). Child welfare agents tend to play down the inexorable nature of the intervention (Hoogsteder et al, 1998) and do not emphasise the client's part in their problems. As a rule, once a court order for intervention has been made, action can be taken promptly and robustly. However, there is always the option to draw back, allowing clients to accommodate 'voluntarily' to the new situation and facilitating their cooperation (Stenson and Watt, 1999).

Family supervisors cannot rely exclusively on their legal authority, but must rather build trust and psychological authority in *face-to-face interactions* with parents and juveniles. Even though clients may be hostile or suspicious and unwilling to cooperate, family supervisors have to establish a relationship that will encourage them to cooperate and accept their advice. Rather than define this relationship in terms of giving and accepting help, it can best be seen as a negotiation.

This is shown in a child welfare case encounter in which a family supervisor (FS) meets the 17-year-old Marco and his parents (van Nijnatten, 2005). At the first meeting, father (F), mother (M) and their son Marco (K) are all present. The boy has been registered at a centre for drug addiction and it has been arranged that he will be admitted there so that he can be cured of the habit.

1. FS: 'Um, first, let's get to know each other, let's begin with you. Can you tell us briefly who you are. I've read the board's report but that's more about what's gone wrong, and of course you are someone other than just what's in that report.'

2. K: 'Yes, well, I'm Marco I'm 16, I'm just 16.'

3. FS: 'Yes, I read that.'

4. K: 'And, well, I've been given a one-year supervision order.'

5. FS: 'Yes.'

6. K: 'And I'm going to the Berg.'

7. FS: 'Yes.'

8. K: 'That's (?) but I could also go to (?).'

9. FS: 'Yes.'

10. K: 'But if I do go to the Berg I would still have to go the home. So, once I've finished at the Berg and my addiction is cured ...'

11. FS: 'Yes.'

12. K: '... then I can come home again and we'll see if everything is going OK by the time I'm 17, if everything is going well. If it isn't going well, the supervision order will be extended.'

The family supervisor tries from the outset to put the boy's identity into a broader perspective. She suggests that the report of the Child Protection Board has probably singled out the negative aspects of the case and that his identity amounts to more than is written there. This is an opening to air any more positive aspects of the boy's character, aspects that are important for any repositioning within the family. He is more than merely a drug addict. The approach is dialogical and enables

Marco to say more about himself. The family supervisor asks the family how they see the nature of the problems. In her eyes, the board's report is an insufficient source of information and she wants to add the client's views. In that way, she tries to ensure that they will understand that their positions are not immutable.

By the time the family supervisor holds a second talk with the parents, Marco has been admitted to the therapeutic centre. She asks the parents to give *their* version of the family history, of 'what actually happened', thus expressing a certain reservation about the contents of the juvenile court's report and indicating that the parents' expertise as witnesses of what actually happened in the family would be appreciated (Potter, 1996). The family supervisor then refers to Marco's admission and finds out how the parents have experienced his departure.

1. M: 'That was a hard day.'

2. F: 'Yes it was a bit, er, that you think ...'

3. M: 'We are so relieved.'

4. F: 'Relieved, yes, because he, er, because of his own feelings too ...'

5. FS: 'Because he rang.'

6. F: 'Yes.'

7. M: 'Yes, that was a huge relief for both of us.'

8. FS: 'Yes.'

9. M: 'Because, because, because he was so nervous on the way, so terribly nervous, it was so emotional saying goodbye that was really awful, I really thought, oh what have I done to him.'

10. FS: 'Yes.'

11. M: 'Yes.'

12. FS: 'Did you think then I'll just take him back again?'

13. M: 'Every time I've // no absolutely not.'

The mother relates that the leave taking was an emotional affair and wonders whether she has taken the right decision. It is noteworthy that the family supervisor twice presents her (alternative) view of the family relationships. In the fifth entry, she attributes the parents' feelings of relief to a telephone call from their son. It seems that the father's relief (4) stems from observing an emotion in his son that reassured him. The mother, however, latches on to family supervisor's interpretation and talks about the emotional leave taking. The family supervisor then suggests that the mother had a hard time letting Marco go (12), something the mother denies categorically. A central question seems to be whether Marco will come back to his parents after treatment or whether he will go to live on his own. The mother allows for both options. According to the supervisor, Marco's wish to return home is an attempt at reconciliation.

1. M: 'Marco is afraid that he'll be homesick if he sees us because on Sunday, he first wanted to ring immediately very understandable.'

2. FS: 'Yes.'

3. M: 'Very understandable.'

4. FS: 'Did you expect that he'd say that?'

5. M: 'I think so, if you see he's really only a child with all his tough talk but he's still just a child.'

6. FS: 'If I were mother, that would do me good to hear him say that.'

7. M: 'Yes, of course, it does us a lot of good.'

8. FS: 'Yes.'

9. M: 'Yes, yes, however it's what I say, it's just an entirely special story, um, we aren't a, er, broken home or anything, through all that stealing look he'd become unmanageable, but later on it's, yes, it's no more, yes, that's all very uplifting, it's ...'

10. FS: 'A new start?'

11. M: 'Yes, how can I say it, yes we can easily make a new start every time afresh.'

12. FS: 'Yes.'

13. M: 'Yes, but this was all necessary, also this supervision order, everything simply necessary in order to shake him awake again.'

14. FS: 'Come on, boy.'

15. M: 'Yes, it's serious it's not all craziness, it's not to torment or to be annoying, it's just you have to …'

16. FS: 'Yes, yes, in the discussion the question was also raised of, um, what they can expect from you two, for instance, suppose Marco wants to come home …'

The mother introduces Marco's anxiety about feeling homesick and for the first time she refers to her son as a child, thereby presenting herself as a parent who knows what a child needs (5). The family supervisor stresses that this is a positive signal in the relationship between mother and son (6). The mother confirms this, but also insists that there is nothing wrong with their family and that her son's problems are his problems alone, and that it was his impossible behaviour that had made him unmanageable (9). Yet, at the same time, the mother says that it does not fully make sense. The positions within the family have shifted. Although the mother defines Marco's addiction as his personal problem, she also sees him as a child (who needs a parent) and asserts that the family is sufficiently resilient to resume responsibility for his upbringing (11) – although not without an order, which she sees as necessary to move Marco in the right direction (13). The supervisor then suggests what the parents might say to their son and uses an expression the parents themselves might have used ("Come on, boy").

After this episode, the family supervisor stresses that if in the future things should get out of hand, they must quickly get together to discuss what is best for Marco. The family supervisor articulates this as a shared task: "Then we'll get together round the table", and "*We'll* just see how *you* think now what is important for Marco, what *we're* going to do". She states clearly that she will not high-handedly intervene but that she wants to know what the parents' position is and hopes that whatever steps are taken, they will undertake them together. This is an example of a sophisticated approach, with the family supervisor combining care and control by simultaneously stressing cooperation (we) and restriction (making a distinction between the parents' views and Marco's interest). Father and mother both wholeheartedly agree, which means that the father is changing his position; what happens has now become a joint responsibility. Yet this is still only a small step because the motive underlying the father's agreement seems to be to prevent his son from coming home again. Father and mother do not expect their son to come home once he leaves the therapeutic institution. The family supervisor emphasises once again that Marco's decision to go into therapy and to stick with it has been taken above all out of loyalty to his parents. She reformulates the parents' remark about Marco failing them. There seems to be agreement when mother admits that Marco, out of a feeling of guilt, probably would not dare look them in the face. The family supervisor appears to succeed in achieving intersubjectivity through the parents' reformulated account of Marco's motives and feelings. The agreement with this new formulation is an important condition for getting some movement in the positions of the parents and the son.

In the fourth conversation, the family supervisor discusses the care plan with the parents. She wants to make sure that the parents really approve of the text of the plan.

1. FS: // but what // what did you find hardest then? you said just as at first // that was very hard

2. F: //(.....?..)// very hard even for him it's very emotional

3. FS: 'You found it completely distressing.'

4. F: 'Yes.'

5. M: 'Distressed the rest of the day.'

6. FS: 'Yes.'

7. M: 'The whole night too.'

8. FS: 'What exactly was so distressing?'

9. M: 'Well, I, I still have the feeling that I've failed or something.'

10. FS: 'Hmm, and that he if he says that ...'

11. M: 'Yes, that's very painful ...'

12. FS: 'Yes.'

13. M: '... that a child has found it so difficult.'

The parents immediately respond positively to the family supervisor's change of direction in the conversation. Initially, in their eyes, the guilt lay with Marco, but now, not only can they express their feelings of distress at seeing their son in such circumstances, but the mother is also able to relate this to her own failure. The mother can put herself in her son's position and for the first time sees that his problems may also be the consequence of problems in the family. She is now capable of detaching Marco's own subjective – with all its associated friction and strife – from her own desires.

1. F: 'It's a good school, a good training for him ...?'

2. M: 'I think it's not only good training for him ...'

3. F: '... and for us too, of course, because I repeatedly learn from things like this.'

4. FS: 'After all, it's not nothing for you to sit here without Marco because he's in Berg?'

5. F: 'It's not pleasant either.'

6. FS: 'No.'

7. F: 'But on one hand it gives you a bit of peace, you know, like these weekends.'

8. FS: 'You are confident, huh // in him // that it'll all come right?'

9. F: '// er, I // I have confidence in it and especially now that the holidays are behind us.'

10. FS: 'Yes that's also true and are you confident?'

11. M: 'Hmm, yes, I'm beginning to get some confidence.'

12. FS: 'Yes, hmm.'

13. F: 'I just think that he, that, er, he'll see it through.'

14. FS: 'Yes he's going to manage it, you think?'

15. F: 'Yes.'

16. FS: 'You see your own // future // fine in a year from now, eh?'

17. F: '// I think // yes, I'd say that and that's why, um, it's the turn for all of us to work for his homecoming, of course, and that.'

By means of a pointed question, the family supervisor raises the question of the parents' expectations regarding the future and explicitly asks them whether they have confidence in it (10). The father says he is confident about the future and that it will be a learning experience for all of them. The mother assents with slight hesitation (11). The family supervisor does not pursue the meaning of this hesitation, but instead presses on to introduce a number of significant reformulations in the dialogue with the father. When the father says that he thinks Marco will see the treatment through (13), she reformulates this as the father thinking that Marco will manage (14), which is a much broader way of construing the outlook. In the next line, she sets a time limit of one year for achieving this (16). The father replies that it is a joint responsibility to work for his son's return home, upon which the family supervisor again refers to the therapeutic sessions, which the father endorses. Both confirm this. The scenario for the future is outlined in a few sentences: if the members of the family agree to participate in these therapeutic sessions, Marco's return home is a realistic possibility within one year.

The family supervisor has succeeded in putting the individual problem of Marco's behaviour into the context of the family and, more significantly, in obtaining the parents' endorsement of this point of view. According to the plan, the parents will get specific support, supervision or treatment as necessary. The strength of the family will have to be gauged again to see whether a placement back in the home will in due course be possible and whether the parents will be able to resume the upbringing of their son without the support of a family supervisor.

Over the course of four conversations, the family supervisor has succeeded in convincing the parents that Marco's problem of drug addiction is not unconnected with the family situation. The relationship between parents and son is now seen as part of the problem and the parents agree with a plan in which they also will be the subjects of supervision.

The conversations analysed here are an exchange of contending arguments rather than a straightforward argument *between* two parties. The result of the conversations is not due to superior argumentation on the part of the family supervisor, but to the joint production of a new understanding of the problem within the family. The family supervisor and the parents have together reached the same point of view: that the parents should look at their son's problems differently from now on. This new understanding of the family dynamics is the end point of a series of collaborations between parents, Marco and the family supervisor. This is not to deny that professional and clients communicate in an asymmetric institutional context in which both authority and empathy are instruments used to achieve the desired changes.

From the very beginning, the family supervisor's approach is directed towards developing a common framework with the parents and juvenile. She does not assume that the court's findings are the only starting point, nor does she pretend that predetermined categories of upbringing, development and addiction are at the root of the problems. Instead, she keeps trying to co-construct a new definition of Marco's problems in terms of family relations. She starts from the idea that you can only make effective changes when these are based on an understanding that is shared by the clients. She lets it be known that different views of reality can co-exist and that she can only work well if she is fully aware, not only of what the juvenile court has judged the situation to be, but also of how the parents and Marco look at the problem and its solution.

This approach is constructive and expressed in tactics and strategies that reveal themselves in the conversations in slight turns of phrasing and reaction. The most frequently used method is to reformulate the contributions from Marco and his parents so as to give them a different 'spin'. These reformulations are presented as supplementary, rather than as corrections, and this seems to have been an important reason for the success of this approach. The family supervisor has taken great care to anticipate how the parents may respond when presenting Marco's problems as, in part, a reaction to other problems in the family. She has tried not to offend the parents or cause unnecessary loss of face. Her reformulations seem on a few occasions to go too far for the parents, and on each such occasion they stress the individual nature of their son's problems. At no time does the family supervisor confront them directly. Sometimes a new formulation is sought while at the same time it is emphasised that parents and children have had to deal with major problems and that the parents have shown considerable courage in carrying on. In this way, the parents are never given the idea that they are guilty of causing their son's problems. At the same time, they are offered the chance of saying that they wish to resume responsibility for his upbringing. By combining a positive and supportive attitude toward the parents with an unrelenting emphasis on the familial character of Marco's problems, the family supervisor has succeeded in getting the parents to reflect on their own position in relation to their son and their share in the problems of his life.

Conclusion

The moment parents get into serious difficulty, once they can no longer manage family life and the children suffer, child welfare gets involved. This may either happen voluntarily, when parents or children appeal to a child welfare agency for help, or coercively when the family court rules that parental authority must be restricted or abrogated. A lack of parental agency results in a professional agency taking over. The goal of child welfare is to enable parents to regain their parental agency as quickly as possible. As long as those families can manage to operate within the parameters of society, and can reflect on their considerations and choices, child welfare exercises restraint. The purpose is not to force families to raise their children according to a particular set of norms, but to foster agency and encourage families to reflect on their situation. Reflection helps parents and children to consider their situation in a more detached way, freeing themselves from the problems that previously imprisoned them. Taking a more distant stance helps them to see things from a different perspective, rather than implying that there is one, and only one, solution to their problems. Such a child welfare strategy requires a dialogical approach.

Dialogical child welfare is a dynamic process, aimed at enabling parents and children to regain control over their life. It is a way of helping clients to negotiate child welfare services. Dialogical child welfare policy nourishes clients' care for themselves as a way to remain autonomous even when they are vulnerable and distressed. Paying attention to clients' narratives fits with the currently felt need that they should be the agents of their lives rather than dominated by pedantic professionalism. These narratives are the outcome of co-constructions based on the biographical expertise of the client and the clinical experience and professional knowledge of the child welfare agent. Seeing things from a different perspective can change clients' lives. Dialogical help is not a question of looking for the single, correct account of their troubles but rather accepting the existence of many stories next to each other, and acknowledging that none of them is a perfect fit. This certainly does not imply that child welfare is not concerned with the moral character of family life. On the contrary, a dialogical approach acknowledges that many moral perspectives on life may exist but is critical of the idea that one should endeavour to conform to an accepted rational norm of family conduct, which can all too easily be presented as neutral and objective. Such an approach would reinforce the weak position of clients as people who have hardly any idea of what a good (family) life might be, but are dependent on others to tell them how to live their lives. Not everybody can live up to the ideal of self-contained autonomy. Rather than taking a dominant position and reinforcing their clients' dependency, the task of care agents is to support these not-so-autonomous people in regaining some control over their lives.

This type of approach makes high demands on child welfare workers. They need a strong professional agency. They have to be able to endure situations of indecision, vagueness and hopelessness without seeking safety in procedures that kill the client's initiatives together with their own uncertainty. Professionals need to be able to present a clearly defined persona and be able to give space to the client rather than make them feel threatened by it. If they can do this, shared understanding may really come about as a co-construction of two types of knowledge, rather than one that has been imposed by the other. In this common frame of action, client and professional understand the central concepts and descriptions without naming them, and they can achieve genuine negotiation about the best steps to be taken. This is a mental process in which, in an enduring relationship, professional and client build common ground where they will find that they can identify the relevant issues much more fruitfully (Edwards and Mercer, 1987).

In this light, it is the responsibility of both child welfare professional and client together to make an all-out effort to reach common formulations about problems in families. Although one can never tell whether parents and child welfare workers really do agree (after all, parental approval may serve a strategic goal, such as preserving a good relationship with the child welfare agent, preventing loss of face, or presenting a positive image (Grossen, 1996)), the primary goal has to be the construction of a common framework in which parents and children can tell their own story and get to grips with the course of events in their family. A relationship is built up in which the connection between the disturbed family processes, the way these are interpreted by child welfare agencies and the plans that are developed to create better conditions to safeguard an authentic development of the child can be agreed. So, even before the problems are solved, parents and children will gain a feeling of continuity as they recognise the problem descriptions and the plans to improve the family conditions. The role of the child welfare agent is to give the family space to construct a family life without the further interference of external agencies, a life that is aimed and limited by the desires of the family members on the one hand and societal rules on the other.

Like other human services, child welfare is a dynamic process of constructing and reconstructing meanings. Child welfare agents help families in trouble to reorganise their lives. The telling and retelling of narratives is mainly a linguistic process, using the symbols of the culture. The professional role of the child welfare worker is communicative, creating psychological space for clients to 'find the words' (van Nijnatten, 2006b). The professional's function is to keep this creative process going and help the client to feel at home in a world that is constantly changing, rather than create certainty by exposing illusory perspectives.

SEVEN

Dialogical management

Government proposes, bureaucracy disposes. And the bureaucracy
must dispose of government proposals by dumping them on us.
P.J. O'Rourke

Any analysis of child welfare needs a discussion about organisation, institutional
agency. In line with the rest of this book, this chapter will analyse child welfare
agencies from a constructivist point of view. In Chapter Five, the negative
evaluations of child welfare were discussed as part of a more overall, neoliberal
protest against the welfare state. Administrations were said to play a too big part
in the provision of welfare, and it was thought to be better to let citizens organise
it themselves. As a result, public human services tried to show that they met
the highest standards, referring more to managerial principles than professional
standards. It was expected that neoliberal organisational models would result in a
market–oriented and therefore less expensive child welfare. Purchasers, customers
and brokers appeared on the market of care. In this chapter, the effect of this new
child welfare policy on dialogical services is studied.

After describing the social mission of child welfare, this chapter goes on to
discuss the rise of a new management culture. Special attention is paid to the
value of management knowledge, the differences between material and immaterial
services and the implementation of free market principles in child welfare. In the
final section, a dialogical approach of management is brought to the fore.

The social mission of child welfare

Ever since the first rationalisation of relief for the poor, child welfare has been
directed at society's deprived communities. Its overall goal has always been to
help marginalised families to regain independence and function without the
support of professional agents and authorities. The rehabilitation and reintegration
function of child welfare has been acknowledged as an essential factor in building
and maintaining social order. In most European societies, state influence on
child welfare is great; this is not surprising, as parental authority is at issue. The
rehabilitation of marginalised people to civilized society has become a major part
of state policy; child welfare is central to this. The strategy in most western societies
is a planned childcare similar to a planned economy. Donzelot (1979) explains
that, just like in Keynes' model, family policy starts from the free enterprise of
parents starting a family and raising children. Keynes linked the two registers of
the production of goods and the production of the producers in a new social

organisation that once started with industrialisation and philanthropy. Just like that, family life was legally embedded (and state controlled) while raising children was still primarily a personal endeavour. Parental agency is the starting point of this policy.

In the same way, child welfare's endeavour is to give parental say back to parents as soon as possible so that they can raise their children without any further interference. This is similar to the objective of family policy and the goal of most parents to raise their children to become autonomous agents. Child welfare only comes into view when the agency of children and/or their parents is seriously at risk. Hence, child welfare policy is successful in the sense that child welfare agents concede the agency of parents and children. However, if child welfare does not succeed in repairing parental authority, it is bound to provide the care children need and so to replace, rather than to repair, family agency. Although children have the right to childcare under the terms of the United Nations Convention on the Rights of the Child, administrations never can guarantee a perfect alternative to bringing up children in their family of origin. Even foster care is only second best. There are means available to deliver various types of social services at parents' and children's request or to impose sanctions on families at risk, but the demand for child welfare can never be predicted completely.

Child welfare is the bridge between the private life of citizens, and accepted norms and societal rules about child rearing, social benefits and education. Child welfare workers apply general rules to individual cases and vice versa – they support marginalised citizens in such a way that they can move again freely in society without putting the social order at risk. Professionals in child welfare agencies occupy a position between the public domain of general rules and the private area of family life. They have an important selective function in determining in which families there is a realistic chance that the developmental conditions of the children will be ameliorated and parental authority restored, and in which families a more coercive intervention is called for. General family policy becomes concrete in personal interpretations of child welfare agents, who tailor interventions to the particular situation of troubled families and at the same time observe commonly accepted social norms and apply neutrality and equality according to the law.

Continuity in child welfare

The task of child welfare is to support continuity in families at risk by repairing or replacing their agency. In a constructive and narrative approach, continuity is considered to be verbal logic. Many child welfare clients lack the verbal capacities to construct continuity by expressing their experiences in words. They are unable to link their past experiences with current and future perspectives, not even when professionals try to help them to express what is going on. This makes child welfare clients more vulnerable and more sensitive to further intervention.

Their lives are in turmoil and what they need most is rest, peace and no sudden changes – in other words, *continuity*.

Does child welfare have the institutional agency to construct this continuity? What is child welfare's socioculturally mediated capacity to act (Ahearn, 2001)? The actions of child welfare agencies are shaped by the social context of the organisation and also reconfigure this context (compare Giddens, 1995). Legal, administrative and (inter)professional contexts of child welfare are crucial for its capacity to act in the best interest of children. Although child welfare interference is a disruption in itself, child welfare agents may contribute to achieving family continuity.

In the US, one of the central methodological goals of child welfare is permanency planning. Permanency is crucial to clients' confidence and their prospects of regaining continuity. Studies in the medical field show that patients acquire more confidence in the quality of medical services after a long-standing relationship with their doctor (Schmittdiel et al, 1997). If they have to conclude frequent contracts with the professional, they are afraid of being unable to create a confidential relationship again. Their uncertainty grows if they hear that they have to change to another doctor. They are anxious that the mutually built knowledge and trust will disappear (Raddish et al, 1999). Over the past few decades, several factors have inhibited child welfare service's continuity. Many professionals are involved with families that have multiple problems: voluntary helpers, general practitioners, the Child Protection Board, judges, police, the child welfare agency, educational professionals. All these professionals and their institutions have their own specific rules and financial systems. The frequent consultations of case managers show the complexity of interprofessional and interagency cooperation and the difficulty in achieving continuity. Differentiation of functions means that clients have to deal with the operator, the intaker, the care agent, the case manager, the behavioural expert, the head of the unit, the manager, and in some cases the members of the complaints committee. Sometimes a file is seen by more than 30 professionals. The advantage is specialisation, the disadvantage is fragmentation. The managerial context of child welfare agencies is crucial for achieving continuity.

Our case study Jennifer met more than hundred such care agents over a period of 15 years. Most of them approached her with an implicit model based on the self-contained individual. Her history has been described and analysed in tens of reports. Cynical as it may be, her file is one of the few continuities in her life. Jennifer alternates between periods of great suspicion about what is written about her and times when she ignores it.

Managerialism in child welfare

The question of how to reduce the costs of the welfare state, rather than the issue of continuity, has dominated the debate about child welfare during the past few decades (Clarke and Newman, 1997). The outcomes of a big American study show that continuity in medical care saves money (Raddish et al, 1999);

the costs of medicines reflect the number of illnesses and hospitalisations and rise with the number of care agents the patient has to deal with. Organisational changes in child welfare agencies are a reaction to the belief that the costs of the welfare state have become too high and that the paternalistic state undermines the citizen's responsibilities (King, 1997). It was felt that those institutions had dealt with their capacities too bureaucratically and acted too remotely from citizens. Organisational changes would have to result in reduced costs and better connection between services and clients' needs. Efficiency and output were the new key words. To achieve this goal, Dutch governmental child welfare institutions became organised and financed at the level of regional public authorities (deregulation). Concomitantly financial risks were reduced. Soon, the new organisations were trying to reduce costs by increasing the scale of their operation. This, again, demanded new rules, extra communication channels and centralised organisation.

Social work (including child welfare) has come under great pressure to legitimate its existence in these new organisations. Referring to a citizen's need for help is no longer seen as sufficient; social work is now required to give an account of its effectiveness in objective, quantifiable terms. Social work has to become an 'actor' in the market of welfare and care, and the government must withdraw because its heavy hand is a distorting factor in the free play of the market (Clarke et al, 2000). It is said that the emphasis on clients' needs has undermined their autonomy and contested the moral character of society; professional bureaucracy would resist necessary transformations and a lack of competition between agencies would resulted in an unlimited need for welfare. A lack of well-defined criteria to measure the effect of social service programmes would confirm lack of productivity. The neoliberal idea is that the problems in child welfare may be solved by new forms of organisation that are thought to contribute to more effective social services that fit better with the changed needs of citizens (Pollitt, 1990). Societal changes demand new skills of citizens and lead to different problems that demand for new types of intervention. Social agents would then be better equipped to operate flexibly and react promptly. Rationalisation was considered to lead to organisational efficiency and a stricter control on expenses. Social services should be modelled on commercial ventures: enterprising, involved, developing and client-oriented. In many areas, indeed, such changes have been realised and this has resulted in a changed relationship between public and private sectors, professionals and managers, and central and local administrations. In practice, different features catch the eye: control, standardisation, client orientation, management style and expertise (compare Clarke and Cochrane, 1998). Below I elaborate on these five features.

Professional entrepreneurship

Professional entrepreneurship aims for efficiency through the introduction of market principles and product financing. In the new management ideology, there is supposed to be a need for dynamic organisations in which partners know how to set about their work and anticipate rapid fluctuations in the market. They govern flexible agencies 'offering choices of non-standardized services; that lead by persuasion and incentives rather than commands; that give their employees a sense of meaning and control, and even ownership' (Osborne and Gaebler, 1992, p 15). The question is whether or not the new management principles go for non-profit services like child welfare. Public officers are not self-employed. Clients have few choices and this child welfare monopoly does not fit with competition between fellow childcare workers.

Benchmarking is often used to introduce competition between welfare agencies. Yet entrepreneurship and free market processes are hard to introduce in non-profit agencies. It is unproven that contract relations support the free market and save money. Yet administrations deliberately put the financial risks with the agencies, so that they can invest less than would have been possible otherwise (Smith and Lipsky, 1993); the attention given to efficiency and saving in costs is disproportionate. 'Entrepreneurs' in child welfare are bound to many forms of state control. Public social services are paid for with government money and are executed within strict rules and regulations of general interest. The ties with these financial, legal and political regulations limit the free movement of public agencies and stimulate bureaucracy. These are all reasons that non-profit agencies cannot be compared with commercial trade and industry just like that.

Child welfare is not only a closed market; its products are also intangible. Its quality cannot be assessed in the same way as it can with tangible products (Bowen and Ford, 2002). A tangible product is literally manipulated; in most cases, a service can only become mental property as a memorable experience. As a product becomes less tangible, its effect is harder to assess, but not impossible. The evaluation is in the head of the client. Child welfare is produced right at the moment that it is consumed and the client participates in the supply and demand process. While tangible products may be checked vigorously and repaired before being presented (again), the quality of child welfare can only be established during the delivery process. Added to that is the fact that the one who delivers the service is in most cases also the one who repairs the defects. That is the reason that service agencies put so much emphasis on the quality of the relationship between the care agent and the client. Care agents should be trained in negotiating and finding acceptable solutions for different kinds of client. They not only have to deliver good services but also contribute to a good relationship with the client and to an open atmosphere in which it is possible for the client to express negative feedback. Professionals in child welfare are not only selected on the basis of skills and output, but on attitude as well.

Control

In the neoliberal paradigm, the ideal is to make the execution of child welfare quantifiable by determining targets and levels of performance, and to advance inspection of the working process. Managers are liable to control the agency's performances. The presupposition is that well-defined goals of performance may be better controlled and so add to quality. A major problem of this approach is that only formal features can be easily made observable and quantifiable formal features, and that emphasis on these formal aspects may lead to neglecting what is more difficult to define precisely. Social services cannot be understood as a number of disparate elements, because the separate elements contribute to the overall significance in the context of the relationship between professional and client. It would be quite easy to measure the time that one spends on the separate parts of child welfare, but much harder, if not impossible, to find out which of these parts contributed to the desired changes. Child welfare is always about ambiguous and sometimes conflicting goals in a context with an uncertain future. A relationship-based strategy might be more effective, as it may respond to the complex situation of clients and their idiosyncrasies in expressing their emotions and negotiating with professionals. It also realises better conditions in which clients' fragmented states of mind can be contained and reflected on (Froggett, 2002). This may lead to a tension between institutional goals of efficient operational management and agents' goals of meeting the client's needs on the basis of professional standards. The primary interest of welfare agencies is their employees performing optimally within the financial margins, whereas the individual child welfare worker wants maximum space to tailor help to his or her client and to deliver professional quality (Lipsky, 1980).

The ideals of 'non-bureaucratic' social service are a paradox of centralisation and decentralisation (Newman, 1998). How is control possible if one lets one's authority slide? Managers of non-profit organisations have a responsibility to operate their services economically and have to try to make policy within these constraints. The new style of management that wants to end bureaucracy puts an emphasis on measurement and so introduces new bureaucratic procedures and actions. Planning and execution can often become separated when planning goes ahead without practitioner input and feedback. This leads to 'missing links' in the chain of information, resulting in extra energy and resources being required to repair this (Lozeau et al, 2002).

Standardisation

Standardisation means that procedures are harmonised. The same procedures are used in different individual cases. A good example is the protocol used in cases of suspected sexual abuse. This protocol encourages the professional to ask certain questions and to seek advice from some people from the network of the client. This helps to prevent important issues from being overlooked, such as medical examination. The use of protocols makes cases more easily transferable between colleagues. In family doctors' practices, the use of standards has been effective in improving professional performance. It also makes the client's position stronger.

There are also problematic sides to standardisation, however. Standardisation puts continuity at risk if it is only used as an instrument to monitor and control employees and clients (Chambers, 1997). It may cause loss of context-specific information. Yet knowledge about the specific needs of parents and children is essential for assessing need and gearing care; knowledge that is reduced to average information that is applicable in any situation and for the 'average' client who may be anybody is of little value. When standards dominate and even overrule clinical expertise, the professional becomes a poll-taker and child welfare a product that might be delivered by anybody. In order to understand the family in its context, child welfare workers need more than a mechanical involvement, and need to find a balance between engagement with the family and professional distance (Cooper and Webb, 1999). One can never predict beforehand what a family needs exactly to overcome their problems. That makes it harder to control employees in a formal way and the chances of having good-quality child welfare are higher in a climate in which the possibilities for good care are optimised, with enough space for the professional to meet with the client's needs: 'Knowledge does not exist in a vacuum as something fixed and packaged, ready to be sold and distributed. This implies a change of focus from an emphasis on formal knowledge to persuasive strategies of convincing all concerned about the expertise and superior rationality one is governed by, and which can benefit the clients' (Alvesson, 2001, p 872).

Client-centred child welfare

In the 1980s, child welfare workers had become more aware of their client's needs, but were still said to behave in a patronising manner. The new ideal was partnership and co-construction. Although child welfare workers aimed at freeing families from their problems, their caring attitude had blinded them to the needs of clients as defined by them. Consequently, child welfare came to be seen as manipulative, and child welfare agents were depicted as the enemies of children's rights and family's rights. The professional identity of social work was questioned. In order to survive this criticism and to maintain its independence from law, social work had to redefine the vocabulary of its profession and reformulate its expertise, a task that was accomplished largely by the imposition of management principles and its associated jargon (compare King, 1997).

The new managerialist way of looking at family problems resulted in a new (more legalistic and distant) manner of assessment. Clients were named customers, and were urged to take control ('empowerment') and to become their own case managers. The agencies consulted their clients to legitimise their policy ('accountability'), inspect the quality of their service and the position of their clients ('monitoring'). Bad work might be displayed in negative outcomes of client satisfaction surveys. But even if the client were displeased with the child welfare service, there would hardly be a real option of going somewhere else. Because of the connection between child welfare services and family law, clients have little choice. Besides, child welfare clients often cannot meet the high standards of cooperation and participation required of them. The strategy of making contracts with clients may seem to be egalitarian, but may in fact put them on the wrong track, because it does not reckon with the disciplinary function of child welfare.

Professional expertise

Professionalism is to reinvent and recreate a tradition of skilful and well-considered operation. Professionalism is about procedures and customs with an immanent value that expresses a certain interest and knowledge related to a professional group with its own professional pride. This is more than just counting goals, means, costs and benefits (Verbrugge, 2004). Management means being enterprising, autonomous, productive, self-regulatory and responsible (Du Gay, 2000). Yet new managerial regulations can also be, or are intended to be, at the cost of professional power, in particular when decision making is thoroughly rationalised, and if the major role of child welfare is control of other professionals rather than providing services (Harris, 1998). On the one hand, the organisation should provide the conditions for the execution of professional expertise; on the other hand, there is growing management control of professionals. Professionals have to be loyal to the institutional principles of bureaucratic precision and budgeting and at the same time meet individual clients' needs (Hjörne et al, 2010). This would seem to be a position full of tension, but when the separate positions are acknowledged in relation to others (the best interest of the child, the institutional goals) this may also encourage change (compare Froggett, 2002). The professional is the very person to take up this position, creating the space clients need to reflect on their difficulties.

Over the past few decades, the organisation of child welfare has changed dramatically. The growing role of managerial principles has permeated the primary process with arguments of pragmatism and objectivism. At the same time, there is a great gap between management and professionals, between control and confidence. Modern managers sometimes have little practical experience and have no idea of the intrinsic value of their 'product'. Yet they claim that they know how to create a competitive and effective organisation. Standards and computers are now a part of child welfare and have changed the relationship between management and professionals in a fundamental way. But this has not resulted in an open market of child welfare, as there is a lack of open competition between various providers. The changes in new public management are only partial (Bovens, 2003), child welfare having developed as a complex mix of old and new elements. The effects of these practices can only be judged on the basis of the implementation process in the political, economic and social context (Newman, 2002). New public management did have a profound influence on professional discretion, but did not get rid of it completely. In fact, in many services, the professional discretion element has been left untouched. Yet in some practices, it has been weakened to the point where the professional works with professional standards but still has clinical freedom of interpretation (Evans and Harris, 2004). Yet Wastell and colleagues (2010) paint a less optimistic picture of child welfare as a professional field that has been overrun by bureaucratic procedures and rules, and is staffed by alienated professionals 'serving in an organisation without much serving it'.

Child welfare professionals have some discretionary freedom, but are also bound to institutional rules in which they have little say (Freidson, 1984), whereas their expertise should be used and their voice be heard (Zeithaml et al, 2006). More institutional control over the content of services may result in less professional freedom (McAuley et al, 2000). The managerial need for precise product description may be an incentive for professionals to account for their activities. Yet bureaucracy becomes counterproductive when it confirms an inconsiderate use of standard procedures. It invites professionals to use double-entry book keeping: giving the official account to management and secretly persevering with unmonitored procedures. Professionals are presented with the task not only of demonstrating their technical skills, but also convincing external subsidisers that their work is cost-effective. In a recent study, Saario and Raitakari (2010) use the concept of performative agency (Dean, 1999) to show how care agents have an active role in proving the effectiveness of their performances. They train themselves to perform in harmony with the local authorities that purchase the services of the agency.

A distinct profile of professionals in child welfare agencies might give a counterweight to managerial bureaucracy. Professional statutes may add to such a profile and prevent regulations from being executed on an individual basis rather than a collective one that emphasises responsibilities, decision-making procedures and operational management. Examples of such professional statutes can be found in hospitals where the representation of clinical specialists is regulated and organised by a medical staff committee (van Dijk and Bruins Slot, 2003). In contrast to the statutes that bind the medical profession, child welfare agents are employees rather than independent contractors. They are bound to the setting of tasks, and in spite of their claim to professional autonomy they are the executors of managerial goals that may be at odds with professional proceedings. Next to meeting the client's needs, the professional has responsibility for gearing these needs to disposable public means. Moreover, the decisions taken by professional employees transcend individual responsibility because the agency discharges the employee, taking institutional responsibility for his or her actions.

The organisation as context for professional child welfare

Organisations can have a positive influence on the quality of child welfare services (Glisson and James, 1992; Glisson, 2002). Important conditions are a dialogical, not a defensive culture, and fewer centralised and formal structures; these add to a safe work context, more involvement, a higher quality of service and fewer referrals to other agencies. As organisational culture and structure contribute to better work attitude and actual outcome, it would be naïve to consider them just as a limitation of professional freedom. The organisation need not take over tasks of the agents, but rather create an atmosphere in which collegiality and structure directed at systemic processes enhance the quality of professional activity. In any organisation, there is a fine balance between control and freedom in the direction of professionals.

A central argument of this book is that the quality of agency depends on its dialogical nature, and that agency develops best in an environment in which the exchange of ideas is encouraged. Hence, the professional's agency also flourishes best in a dialogical work environment. Moreover, dialogical child welfare agencies perform better if they can function in a society that is responsive and does not turn away from a dynamic interchange of ideas and views.

Recent devastating criticisms of Dutch child welfare as a result of systemic failures leading to fatalities may stem from feelings of paranoia; a similar reaction can be seen in analogous situations in the UK. Some clients, journalists and politicians believe that child welfare has to be perfect (meaning that it should prevent calamities) and if it does not, then it is bad. The immediate, standard reaction to the news of a child being killed by his or her parents is that child welfare has failed. This may be an unconscious strategy to safeguard parenthood as a natural, good quality by not blaming the parents, but it is also stems from the difficulty people have in accepting that in a society in which parents – within societal limits – have the freedom to have children and raise them in whichever way they like, child welfare can only react to, or try to prevent, problems. Child welfare cannot be perfect and to demand perfection leads to a paranoid agency in which professionals are pressed to work harder, prove more and set higher standards. This is in itself no problem as long as there is a realistic possibility of improving child welfare services.

Yet there are signs that the principles of the 'free market' and standards of 'evidence base' lead to rivalry and agencies bidding against other agencies. Politicians and managers try to sift the wheat from the chaff, for instance by benchmarking. The idea is that this will stimulate agencies to work harder and meet higher standards, but the reality is that organisations spend more time on impression management than on service delivery. It leads to a monomaniac subjection to the magic question 'What works?' and is based on the supreme belief that there is a solution to every problem and that clients can always be convinced and moved to change. This type of 'macho management' is a search for personal success that functions as a defence against the uncertainties of life in general and of child welfare families in particular rather than a vision of what *can* be done (Froggett, 2002). It seems hard to be reconciled to the fact that social sciences and social agencies lack the ultimate answers for how to deal with the unpredictability of reality. Mundane reality is often unruly for even the most modern welfare programmes. But the ongoing search for perfection that hides basic insecurities about what is possible is at the heart of splitting processes in agencies and society, and makes professionals more receptive to their client's projections. Moreover, it makes them sympathetic to new case management procedures that keep emotions and uncertainties at bay. Such a 'professional' attitude kills creativity and ignores the fact that an acceptance of reality is necessary in helping clients to concede that an imperfect life is still very much worth living: 'An over-evaluation of efficiency may be allied to delusions of infinite perfectibility which operate as a defence against disappointment. This is the shadow side to a performative culture that defines itself in concepts of continuous development, lifelong learning, change and growth' (Froggett, 2002, p 127).

Directing professionals

Child welfare agencies are professional organisations, characterised by systematic performances within the framework of an acknowledged occupation. The concept of skill (professional competence) is central. Professional performance adds in considerable measure to the quality of child welfare. Some see professional competency as no more than cognitive achievements usable in any welfare situation. Such an approach does not acknowledge the influence of interpersonal relationships, the division of knowledge and the cultural context of professional work (Holman, 2000). Professionalism is not just the execution of the correct rules or the utterance of magic words; that would be a unilateral action that ignores the client. Co-construction and tuning of meanings should be at the heart of professional child welfare. Standards should take into account the views of clients and avoid a situation where clients just answer predetermined questions; to do the latter would be to admit that clients have no control over their lives even before there has been any contact with them. To take such an approach is to ignore the clients' perspectives on their lives. At any time, clients may accept or deny the interpretations and actions of the child welfare agent. In their encounters, clients and professionals negotiate about, and make sense of, meanings. The challenge for the professional is negotiate with each client rhetorically and tactfully to achieve common knowledge and shared decision.

A good (enough) professional knows how to find the middle road between technical performance and the use of standardised tools and procedures, and attention to the specific and unpredictable aspects of real-life situations. The use of protocols and standards is helpful for a dialogical approach, as long as it supports a significant exchange of meanings between client and professional. If not, it will result in technical tours de force that only serve to upgrade the social status of the profession. The use of standard forms presupposes certain outcomes in certain situations, for example, in the Dutch selection committee system for making decisions about placements in children's homes. These placements were originally 'arranged' through personal contacts, but selection committees were thought to be fairer and to result in better use of vacancies in residential institutions; in fact, they have proved to be bureaucratic millstones that make rapid decisions impossible.

Excessive attention to formal procedures easily leads to a superficial approach that detracts from common understanding and change of meaning. If, for institutional reasons, professionals have to perform only within a framework of testable qualities, their discretionary freedom to act in a professional way is unnecessarily reduced: 'For the convenience and control of normal professionals, it is not the local, complex, diverse, dynamic and unpredictable reality of those who are poor, weak and peripheral that counts, but the flat shadows of that reality that they, prisoners of their professionalism, fashion for themselves' (Chambers, 1997, p 55). Now, the professional has three possibilities. The first is to use double-entry book keeping of testable results to appease management, while continuing to deal with clients in an informal way. The second and third options are for the professional to associate with just one of the parties. If the child welfare agent follows institutional rules, the chances are high that the performance loses its reflexive and responsive character and that the client will be unhappy with the outcomes. From a professional point of view, many child welfare workers will have difficulty working like this; it may also end in burn-out, especially with idealistic young workers (Freidson, 1984). Conversely, if workers concentrate solely on the dialogical character of their work, they risk coming into conflict with management.

But are these three options exclusive? In the rest of this chapter, I will discuss a fourth option in which management and primary processes relate to each other in a dialogical tension rather than in opposition.

Dialogical agency

Dialogue is not only crucial for the development of individual and interactive agency in the private lives of citizens, but is also fundamental in nurturing and repairing relationships. The same goes for professional workers and institutions. Just as children can only accomplish interactive agency in an environment dominated by dialogical caregivers, so professional helpers will only achieve good interactive professionalism in a dialogical working environment. How can such a dialogical professional context be advanced?

Over the past decade, authors of the American Taos group published the outcomes of their research in the field of dialogical organisation (Anderson and Burney, 1996; Anderson et al, 2001; Gergen et al, 2004). Their starting point is that as human reality is constructed in relationships and through dialogue, people only become motivated if the organisation can organise a meaningful dialogue. This meaningful dialogue is the basis for coordination, harmony and growth of meaning (Anderson et al, 2001). Dialogue helps professionals to feel and act responsibly, coordinate their actions and take a reflexive and affirmative attitude towards their work. It also makes it easier to exchange disconnection and opposition for common enterprise and cooperation (Gergen et al, 2001). Chapter Six of this volume concluded that responsive organisation needs a kind of sanctuary in which the subjectivity of the professional is made effective rather than neutralised. This enables both professionals and clients to distance themselves from their direct experiences and consider them from afar. It is therefore essential that dialogical processes are facilitated in organisation; these processes are based on, and are the basis for, an approach of openness, respect, curiosity about and connection with the other. In such an environment, employees have the capacity to act, or believe that they can do so, and are able to cope with their dilemmas in a competent and autonomous way. In the process of new meanings and narratives that are exchanged among employees, individual-agency emerges (Anderson and Burney, 1996). Organisations are nets of collective action undertaken in an effort to shape the world and human lives. Organisa*tion* is an activity rather than a resulting object (Czarniawska, 1997, p 41).

In order to support the dialogical character of child welfare, it is necessary to organise planning and control in a dialogical way. That means that room is organised between child welfare agents and clients and between colleagues themselves to allow them to discuss their deeper thoughts, hopes, fears, ambitions and feelings of powerlessness together. Intake, assessment, guidance and completion are then primarily considered as dialogical processes. The child welfare agent is expected to have discussion with clients about the problems and solutions in their family. It is considered to be useful that the client's perspectives are seen in multiple perspectives and that these different perspectives are based on the positions taken by those involved. The crux of the problem only becomes clear in the course of the meetings between care agent and client.

In what ways can management support dialogue in child welfare? How can they create an area that is dominated by professional creativeness rather than institutional principles? The agency can create room by distancing itself in setting specific organisational and bureaucratic situations and by actively encouraging a reflexive culture. Child welfare agents may be stimulated to enter such a relationship with the client in four different ways. These are outlined below.

Encouraging a dialogical culture between colleagues

In the dialogical organisation, emphasis is put on primary processes where the professional's voice can be heard. Supervision was pre-eminently a dialogical way of allowing novice employees to put their professional principles into practice. Although reflexive questions such as 'How do you feel about this?' are often sneered at as being the province of woolly liberalism, this type of question used to help social workers to look critically at themselves and at the effectiveness of their performance. More important than the matter of horizontal or vertical regulation – in many child welfare agencies, by senior professionals has been substituted by peer supervision – is the issue of how to organise. Supervision used to be undertaken by the practice supervisor, who then allocated responsibilities with regard to professional standards and had an important function in performance interviews. Peer supervision has to be organised by the professionals themselves, but facilities and time are limited. In a professional service, an open dialogue between experienced and non-experienced professionals is necessary.

Such an open dialogical culture is not easy to organise and requires an unconventional management approach, as, for example, with Mannoni's (1976) approach in Bonneuil, a therapeutic clinic near Paris. This school caters for children with social and psychological problems. According to Bonneuil policy, when a child 'sponges off' co-residents, the professional's task is to try to help the child put his or her lack of individual agency into words. It is important that the *child* expresses what might be lacking or missing such that he or she should find it necessary to take advantage of co-residents, partly because the adult does not pretend to cater for the child's needs. The differences between adults and children are not disguised at Bonneuil, so the children learn to deal with the different lines that are drawn by different adults. Adults cannot fall back on predetermined diagnoses or plans – there are no case conferences in which information about children is gathered, no files and no treatment plans – but adults are asked to undertake activities with the children because they want to do so. There are weekly meetings without an agenda where adults are given the space to make suggestions, verbalise their feelings towards the children and to clarify their personal involvement in particular cases.

Similar meetings are organised in the French psychotherapy clinic, La Borde, in which 'constellations' of people are gathered around a patient not on the basis of professional status but because they themselves choose to discuss issues of conflict and differences of opinion with the patient. Ledoux (2004), a psychotherapist in attendance at La Borde, states that classical psychiatry excludes patients by emphasising treatment plans, personal files and 'care communication'. In the dialogical approach, the professional has to ensure that the patient's file is uniform and that the treatment plan has clear goals that act as directives for treatment staff. Such institutional routine prevents one from looking for what is left unspoken. According to Ledoux, the spoken word is uncontrollable and hard to confine, and always raises new dimensions ('dit-mension') in which the unspoken is relevant. That is why classical psychiatry wants to replace the spoken word by documents that control the unspoken through clearly defined objectives. At La Borde, this approach was challenged by inviting employees at staff meetings to exchange thoughts around patients and, if possible, to investigate their own powerlessness more deeply. To everybody's surprise, these meetings resulted in noticeable changes in the patients' conduct. The radical policies in Bonneuil and La Borde are far from the professional practices we are used to and may seem chaotic, but nothing is further from the truth. In fact, the professionals are trained to mark out their own limits daily and to create room in which children can live their life on their own terms, recognising the limits of others rather than being extensions of adults who do not accept their limited position. Each organisation should try to create an 'inner space where the symbolization is tolerated, enabled and even encouraged, and where people can express something of their own subjectivity' (Arnaud and Vanheule, 2007, p 13).

According to Andersen (cited in Griffith, 1999), members of 'reflexive teams' in case conferences aim at finding a balance between observing and participating roles. The goal is to gather all perspectives. This is possible by alternating between questioning, listening and reflective roles in collegial meetings. This demands that professionals create room for their colleagues' positions without seeing them as a threat to their own positions. It also requires them to wait a while before giving their own opinions and to ask for the opinions of colleagues. Transitional conditions are necessary to enable one to stop being the object and become aware that one is an active agent (Mannoni, 1979). The emptiness of the transitional space plays an important role in the transfer from being an object into having an object (as a subject), and to gain control. In a dialogical approach, professional performance is a social achievement (Holman, 2000). Of course, child welfare workers cannot afford to finish case conferences without a plan or conclusion; they are legally bound to prepare or take decisions about the status of the client. Yet a well-considered answer seems more probable if professionals consider their colleagues' different and conflicting views rather than follow a particular institutional line. This helps them to go beyond standard answers and to come to a good decision by considering different positions and points of view.

Giving professionals adequate time and space for dialogue

It is management's task to distribute benefits and costs in such a way that institutional goals are achieved. This implies that the institution establishes the optimum time allocated to each client. The amount of time allowed for primary processes depends on how much time management deems necessary. The organisational costs involved often rise more rapidly that the costs of the primary processes themselves.

Granting child welfare workers professional freedom

Child welfare agencies should be guided by professional rather than institutional standards. In some agencies, the primary process is colonised by bureaucracy. Managers have increased the amount of control they have over employees by requiring them to complete detailed time sheets for all tasks and then using the information to draw up normative timetables. By 'chopping and dicing' professional work into numerous fragments, it is possible to calculate how much a task takes and determine an optimum time investment per activity. This is of questionable benefit, because only when they are part of an overall process can these elements acquire any meaning and their contribution be estimated. A certain amount of managerial restraint seems appropriate; quality systems, strategic planning and new ways of accounting are often counterproductive if they are introduced top down and can overlook the link with the families the professionals have to work with. It is more effective to acknowledge the diversity of the client population and allow professionals leeway (within institutional limits) in their encounters with clients. Professional agents will never escape the dialectic of their status as professional employees, who are loyal to both institutional and professional guidelines. It is the professional's task to harmonise these two elements in daily practice (Hjörne et al, 2010). Yet it is not their exclusive responsibility to balance the tension between demand and supply. It may be better for this tension to come into the open, so that client and institution are aware of their positions. Tipping the scale too far in the client's direction might lead to a neglect of the professional's function – in this case, the protection of minors. Tipping the scale too far in the other direction would prevent a real exchange of ideas and only lead to feigned adaptation. It is the task of management to make the professional aware of this tension and to give them space to use it when reflecting on their work.

Promoting dialogue and reflection between managers and professionals

Promoting dialogue and reflection between managers and professionals means that, at certain times, managers have to encourage or conserve bottom-up processes, and at others times to stay aloof. Simpson and colleagues (2002) use the term 'negative capability', which is the art of not intervening, or staying inactive. As discussed earlier, it means 'containing', which is the capacity to absorb negativity rather than confronting it; in other words, it is the ability to contain difficult situations without returning the problem. Negative capability is the skill of doing nothing, the refusal to defend oneself against criticism. Leadership is usually described in terms of positive capabilities – taking relevant decisions and doing the right thing. In difficult circumstances, there may be great pressure on managers to act, to solve problems. Although negative capability is not always the solution, in certain circumstances it may be more helpful to refrain from making immediate decisions. Employees then get the chance to experience the problems and to use their creativity to find a solution. It may take some effort to let the uncertainty have its moment and to give new ideas a chance. Managers need the ability to wait and observe instead of acting directly. Human management is about hearing symptoms rather than curing them (Arnaud and Vanheule, 2007). This may help make a creative space in which employees can discard their role as docile executors of managers' commands and take an active role as professional subjects. It is the art of resisting the tendency to undo uncertainty with new narratives.

Room for the exchange of ideas and contemplation does not necessarily result in managers staying remote from what is happening on the shopfloor. The idea is that managers *do* show their involvement in the quality of the services. This enlarges the professionals' confidence and helps them to get their breath back. Such a relationship between management and primary process fits with the philosophy of 'self-management' and belonging forms of 'accountability'. If managers give child welfare agents more leeway to fulfil their tasks according to their personal professional standards, accountability gets more and more important. In self-managing teams, individual workers get more responsibility. To guarantee a professional standard, the institution has to trust the individual accounts of its employees. This is only possible if professionals go beyond a solipsistic attitude, seeking acknowledgement of their individual performance, and look for shared values that are objectified in professional experience and standards. Such an 'accountability' nurses the manager's appreciation of the complexity of human services, and increases the employee's understanding of managerial problems. This, again, may foster confidence between professionals and managers. If professionals are convinced that the managers are sincerely interested in the progress of their work, they are more open to scrutiny. This presupposes a culture of respectful accord based on open dialogue rather than unilateral control by formal systems. Sound professional accounts reduce the need for external procedures and enlarge mutual trust (Thoms et al, 2002). This process between managers and professionals develops alongside the process between professionals and clients, in which the challenge is to combine perspectives on the client's life rather than the professional commanding the client what to do.

Conclusion

Previous chapters have described how, over the course of time, parenthood has changed and parents have adopted a facilitating approach in bringing up their children, considering them as negotiating partners. Child welfare interventions have developed in a similar way, with professionals trying to help clients to become autonomous again. Child welfare also demands a facilitating approach from the child welfare worker, whose role it is to make the client's voice audible. Earlier chapters advocate a dialogical child welfare that honours the client's frame of reference. Significant help only seems possible within such a framework. A similar facilitating approach has been advocated for the way in which child welfare managers treat their employees. Child welfare managers have a great impact on the quality of services; they steer the primary process and determine how much discretion individual workers are given. The dialogue is central to good management in child welfare.

The past few decades have seen disparate developments. On the one hand, professionalism has increased, while on the other, child welfare agencies have become more hierarchical. In reaction to the so-called failures of social work, many managers are oriented exclusively to controlling output and reducing the scope of professional discretion. The introduction of new protocols, educational programmes and consultation strategies may be presented as being in the interests of professionals but rather serve as safeguards for managers. Management is so self-centred, so convinced of its powers that one may even detect 'institutional narcissism', reflected in the trend for publishing annual reports, increasing expenditure on public relations and designing new logos. There seems to be an almost infinite belief in the ability of management to create the perfect organisation. Management is for winners; there is no room for uncertainty or doubt. This type of management may be called imaginary; its convictions compensate for the insufficiency of subordinates and it allows no room for divergent views.

Such an approach fails to recognise that the management at most creates the conditions for employees to execute services and is never a goal in itself. There is a risk that management values will end up permeating the professional arena and forcing professionals to translate and reduce complex client situations into simple, scheduled decisions and to manage their clients rather than to help them. Too much attention to organisational matters may lead to defensive reactions; for instance, with regard to professional quality, discussions about what is good (enough) may degenerate into what is sound according to the rules. The new managerial culture is often presented as a victory over the costly welfare culture of the 1970s in which social workers were said to have done no more than to sway with their clients. But much was lost by the new management style. Dialogue with clients came under pressure as professionals needed more time for reporting, evaluation and accounting, while doubts were replaced by rapid decisions. The encounter between client and professional lost much of its significance, whereas it had once been seen as the starting point for potential change in a client's position.

Vulnerability rather than an emphasis on rules and procedures is the basis of social work (compare Smith, 2001). The same goes for institutional relations in which vulnerability confirms collegiality, because it results in mutual trust between colleagues rather than dependence on the structure of the organisation. Dialogical management offers a different view on the organisation of welfare, in that it is necessary for managers to inspire confidence, both in agents and their clients. Moreover, managerial certainty is not guaranteed. As professional employees become more responsible for the implementation of the agency's mission and rely less on external consultants as catalysts, the organisation becomes empowered to act as its own agent of change (Anderson et al, 1996). This is similar to processes in child rearing and child welfare, where success also depends on the respective participation of children and families.

EIGHT

Dialogical child welfare: conclusion

Maybe that's what writing is all about. Not recording events from
the past, but making things happen in the future.
Paul Auster

In this book, I have discussed the function of dialogue in development, the
upbringing of children, child welfare and child welfare organisation. I started from
the idea that words –spoken and written – enable people to build up psychological
continuity. Words are instruments that give structure to constantly changing life
conditions. But this continuity also has a social context, and a society is only a
social order if its members speak more or less in the same culturally accepted way,
producing a common sense. This common ground is the foundation of social
institutions. Continuity is then a social and narrative construct rather than an
exclusively psychological one. People construct their life by telling stories about
their life and by the active role they assume in the telling; they represent themselves
to others and by doing so they define and redefine themselves. Continuity is thus
the outcome of dialogical processes in which images of the self are presented and
represented. In speaking, people affirm their subjectivity and their bond with
the cultural context in which they live and the language they speak. Because
language is symbolic, it is fundamentally symbols that enable people to take a
subjective position towards others, and create shared understanding of the world
they are involved in.

This shared understanding is often missing or is only rudimentary in families that
have lost their grip on life and have become dependent on child welfare. In the
most extreme cases, their lives are characterised by chaos, break-up and disorder.
Parents and children make frantic efforts to free themselves from the chain of
discontinuities, but often the seeds of these discontinuities have been sown at an
earlier stage and are apparent in their life choices; perhaps they have married and
had children at a young age, have had numerous, short-lived relationships, or take
drugs or gamble to avoid facing their difficulties. It is sometimes a torment of
Tantalus that can last for generations, an ongoing combination of negative social
and individual factors that get them into trouble, and through which they then
lose their independence. In many child welfare families, however, the situation is
less desperate and child welfare intervention may be successful within a relatively
short time.

Agency is one of the central concepts in this book. The term 'individual
agency' refers to the power of people to run their own lives, their authenticity
and autonomy in making a life for themselves. But 'agency' can also refer to

mediation; people can get things done through the efforts of intermediaries. Child welfare workers have an important intermediary function. Finally, 'agency' refers to public organisations or institutions. The concept of agency at the three levels of individual development, interaction and social structure are interrelated. If the agency of a family, parent or child is at risk, professional agency is needed to fill this lack. In this book, I have analysed child, welfare and agency at all three levels, arguing that they are interdependent. A central concept in this account of child welfare is the *dialogical* nature of individual, professional and organisational agency. Dialogue is the very instrument by which to try to realise *continuity* and to get a new sense of meaning and meaningfulness.

I have discussed individual and social factors that lead to discontinuity and to the restoration of continuity. I have emphasised that the individual development of children is a social process rather than an essential quality; that is, infants start their lives without a psychological operational system and are completely dependent on the help of significant others to organise their early lives. In their relationship with these others, they develop individual agency and gain the power to structure their lives. Human development has a dialogical basis, with children learning to structure their lives by understanding the world in communication with others. The child constructs unique historical positions from which to take position with regard to other people and to build up agency. This is never a perfect control of self, because both the sense of 'I' and the position towards others are alien rather than essential. If we want to understand the problems of child welfare families, we have to fathom the deficits in the processes of constructing meanings and how these deficits have led to discontinuity.

For children to develop individual agency, they need an environment that is both receptive and limiting. Children need to feel free to explore the world and to undertake new actions; in this journey, they learn their subjective position by being limited by other people. Parenting is therefore both a process of recognition and limitation of the child's willpower. In the relationship with his or her parents, the child also develops interactive agency. Children learn to become active participants in all kind of daily communicative situations. Finally, the developmental perspective of children is determined by their social identity. Children and their families are defined by various social categories, which can facilitate entry into society, or, on the contrary, block access to all kind of social services and provisions. The upbringing of children is influenced by social conditions and historical and cultural changes in society. The social context of families in modern society has resulted in radical changes in the composition of families, the quality of relationships and parenting styles. Nowadays, although many more people outside the family are involved in the upbringing of children, this is in no way a unique situation. Historically speaking, the nuclear family is the exception rather than the rule. What remains unchanged is parental responsibility for the care and raising of their children.

One of the loftier ambitions of current western societies is the autonomy of their citizens; and yet it is the dominance of such values as self-containment, free choice and negotiation that push some people to the margins of society. Citizens who cannot live up to these standards become the object of (coercive) care and social support.

Child welfare investigates the quality of care and upbringing of children in families at risk, deciding on the basis of this assessment whether or not a legal intervention in the family is required. Some experts in the field of child welfare emphasise that these assessments should be based on scientific evidence. Although it is self-evident that the judgements of family courts and child welfare agencies should be based on the best information available, these experts assume that objective evidence and rigorous procedures for data collection are the most accurate way of assessing how parents and children function in the context of their family. But it is not at all obvious that this kind of evidence-based knowledge, which now predominates in the field of child welfare, *is* the best available. It can, in fact, be misleading, as it often leads to a description of families in terms of individual competencies that are divorced from the complex of family interactions and changing society. Such an approach leads to loss of relevant information that is bound to the specific societal and family contexts in which the child is raised. I consider that assessment should be an interactive and contextual process in which family members and professionals try to come to a shared understanding of what is going wrong in the family, and how they should face these difficulties.

Assessment is also a dialogical process in which elements from different perspectives are co-constructed through negotiation and fine-tuning, rather than an application by external agencies of standards that have been constructed in the laboratories of science and have no meaning in the context of the client. The assessment becomes more significant when justice is done to the different perspectives on the family problems. There is never one, exclusively 'true', account of the family's experience that has to be established in order to make the one sound decision. If the clients can themselves identify with the descriptions in the report submitted to the family court, there is more chance that the clients will understand the nature of the family problems and want to cooperate to find a solution to them. In that case, the assessment is already the initial impetus to finding a different view of the family's situation. The uncertainty of the diagnostic process is analogous to the ambiguity of the family's future. By approaching parents and children as active communicative partners in the assessment procedure, the child welfare agent tries to encourage the client to break out of their spiral of passive self-victimisation in the face of all kinds of problems.

Of course, any official report of a family's problems is a reduction of their situation and can never do full justice to the complexity of families. It is rather one stage in the interactive process between family and child welfare that attempts to bring together two worlds of meaning and to get people to move on. A reflective approach on the part of the child welfare worker creates space in which ambiguity and uncertainty can exist and clients can look for words that help them to move. The client's contributions are proof of their agency.

Child welfare is a dynamic process of constructing and reconstructing meanings. The professional's function is to keep this creative process going, helping the client to feel at home in a world that is constantly changing, rather than creating certainty through illusory perspectives. Dialogical child welfare helps families to take a different view of their situation and create a life without external intervention. First, dialogical child welfare helps clients to find the words they need, to tempt them to enter into a dialogue with the professional, and to teach them that none of the plans, stories or perspectives they negotiate can ever be a perfect fit. Such negotiation takes time. This approach does not and cannot result in a distant or neutral stance. On the contrary, a dialogical approach accepts that living life is a moral venture rather than a rational and technical exercise. The task is to keep open an exchange of ideas and ideals between client and professional and to try to reach a common conclusion about what is the best thing to do. If child welfare wants to be more than just an inventory of fragments, the processes of meaning construction have to serve as a guide. This seems to be the only way to find shared ground with the client and help him or her to (re)integrate into society. Only when the client's voice is heard can there be a realistic chance of effective help.

Professionals in child welfare do not act purely as individuals; they function within a qualifying context. In other words, a dialogical approach on the part of child welfare families also needs a dialogical approach on the part of child welfare agencies. Accordingly, I argue for a facilitating institutional culture in child welfare agencies. This calls for special institutional conditions, as dialogue and reflection require an open organisation in which the interactions between professional and client and between manager and professional serve as a starting point rather than acting as predetermined procedural rules for the controlled fabrication of a 'product'. The management of professionals is a fine balance between discretionary freedom on the one hand and adherence to professional standards and institutional conditions on the other. It demands involvement in an open dialogue in which management and professionals meet in the same way as professional and client. The professional is as vulnerable in relation to the manager as the client is to the professional. Management should be facilitating and should never become a goal in itself.

The task of child welfare is to make every effort to restore continuity in troubled families. This book is an argument for refocusing attention on dialogue in child welfare. Only in and through conversations between clients and child welfare workers does it become possible to develop new visions for the lives of these families. Dialogical child welfare means that the voices of both the client and the child welfare worker matter. The aim of dialogical child welfare is to realise changes by addressing the client's agency from the start rather than making an assessment and starting up a programme of help that primarily would reinforce the client's dependence. In my view, child welfare has to be constructive, and I am critical of efforts to reduce it to a kind of intervention that can be wheeled into action in any situation. Constructive child welfare takes a critical stand against so-called 'truths' that are presented concerning clients and their ways of living.

Special attention is paid to the social context in which clients live and clients' perceptions of that reality. In this view, child welfare is a process of the construction and reconstruction of meaning, and an effort to restore and guarantee continuity in the life of clients. In that sense, this book is a response to the policy of control that currently dominates child welfare in western countries.

In this book, I have argued that the condition of child welfare families cannot be known from the outside. Family members only betray their secrets if they are approached as rational subjects who are able to make meaning of their lives. No adequate assessment can be gained by treating families as weak-willed objects to be studied objectively. Dialogical child welfare starts by acknowledging the agency of all participants: the child, the parent, the child welfare worker, and his or her manager. These people may start from different perspectives but have to try to reach common ground, respecting each other's positions rather than starting from hierarchical position where one has supremacy over the other.

Finally, this book is about continuity and discontinuity in development and parenthood, and child welfare's attempts to restore continuity. A constructivist and dialogical view of child welfare goes hand in hand with a critical and problematising approach with regard to the 'facts' about people's lives and relationships. People construct their interpretations of reality in daily interactions, such as with their child welfare agent. That is why in this book special attention is paid to the dialogical character of the helping relationship. The first involvement with child welfare is the beginning of a period defined by new breaches and interventions. This alternation of continuity and discontinuity is also a central theme. There is no single solution for all family problems, professional difficulties or organisational dilemmas. The pursuit of perfection is pointless and may create further problems rather than solving them. In the end, this book is no more than an imperfect contribution to a better child welfare. But knowing that perfection is not feasible does not relieve us of the task and responsibility of trying. This can best be done by opening the dialogue about child welfare and going on to discuss all the many aspects of it.

Most families that are involved with child welfare services have a long, drawn-out history of aggression, relationship break-ups and traumas that are repeated from generation to generation. The journey through child welfare is often long and does not always lead to complete recovery. Many families live in a state of permanent dependency in which parental authority is controlled or taken away completely. Society cannot remain aloof when parents are unable to take care of their children; it must take over that responsibility and to do its utmost to preserve what good is left between parents and children.

Development is synonymous with the acquisition of cognitive, social and emotional competencies, but is also far more than that. Parents can never claim that their influence on their children's development has come to and end. Parenting is an open engagement with children who are dependent on their parents and want to learn from them. The core of any parental enterprise is the belief and the confidence that life is worth living. Parental authority is based on the right –

perhaps even the obligation – of the parent to appeal to the child in the name of his or her beliefs. If the parents do not succeed to do this, it is the task of society to challenge the child to search for the good life. Merely by surviving their birth, children show that they want to live. It is sometimes a miracle that children like Jennifer still want to live after what they have been through. That is the best starting point for any welfare.

References

Achterhuis, H. (1980) *De markt van welzijn en geluk. Een kritiek van de andragogie* (*The market of welfare and happiness. A critique of andragogy*), Baarn: Ambo.

Adamson, L., Bakeman, R. and Deckner, D. (2005) 'Infusing symbols into joint engagement: developmental themes and variations', in L. Namy (ed) *Symbol use and symbolic representation: Developmental and comparative perspectives*, Mahwah, NJ: Lawrence Erlbaum, pp 171-95.

Ahearn, L. (2001) Language and agency, *Annual Review of Anthropology*, vol 30, pp 109-37.

Alvesson, M. (2001) 'Knowledge work: ambiguity, image and identity', *Human Relations*, vol 54, pp 863-86.

Anderson, H. (2002) 'In the space between people: Seikkula's open dialogue approach', *Journal of Marital and Family Therapy*, vol 28, pp 279-81.

Anderson, H. and Burney, J. (1996) 'Collaborative inquiry: a postmodern approach to organizational consultation', *Human Systems. The Journal of Consultation and Management*, vol 7, pp 171-88.

Anderson, H. and Goolishian, H. (1992) 'The client is the expert: a not-knowing approach to therapy', in S. McNamee and K. Gergen (eds) *Therapy as social construction*, London: Sage Publications, pp 25-39.

Anderson, H., Cooperrider, D., Gergen, K., Gergen, M., McNamee, S. and Whitney, D. (2001) *The appreciative organization*, Chagrin Falls, OH: Taos Institute Publications.

Arnaud, G. and Vanheule, S. (2007) 'The division of the subject and the organization: a Lacanian approach to subjectivity at work', *Journal of Organizational Change Management*, vol 20, pp 359-69.

Bakhtin, M. (1986) *Speech genres and other late essays* (translation by V. McGee), Austin, TX: University of Texas Press.

Barker, C. and Galasinski, D. (2001) *Cultural studies and discourse analysis. A dialogue on language and identity*, London: Sage Publications.

Barthes, R. (1977) *Fragments d' un discours amoureaux*, Paris: Editions du Seuil.

Bauer, J. and Bonanno, G. (2001) 'Continuity and discontinuity: bridging one's past and present in stories of conjugal bereavement', *Narrative Inquiry*, vol 11, pp 123-58.

Baumrind, D. (1968) 'Authoritarian versus authoritative parental control', *Adolescence*, vol 3, pp 255-72.

Baumrind, D. (1978) 'Reciprocal rights and responsibilities in parent-child relations', *Journal of Social Issues*, vol 34, pp 179-96.

Beck, U. (1992) *Risk society: Towards a new modernity*, London: Sage Publications.

Bendle, M. (2002) 'The crisis of "identity" in high modernity', *British Journal of Sociology*, vol 53, pp 1-18.

Benjamin, J. (1990) *The bonds of love. Psychoanalysis, feminism, and the problem of domination*, London: Virago Press.

Berger, P. and Luckman, T. (1971) *The social construction of reality*, Harmondsworth: Penguin Books.

Bertau, M. (2004) 'Developmental origins of the dialogical self: some significant moments', in H. Hermans and G. Dimaggio (eds) *The dialogical self in psychotherapy*, Hove and New York, NY: Brunner-Routledge, pp 29-42.

Biesta, G. (2007) 'Why "What works" won't work: evidence-based practice and the democratic deficit in educational research', *Educational Theory*, vol 57, pp 1-22.

Boutellier, H. (2002) *De veiligheidsutopie. Hedendaags onbehagen en verlangen rond misdaad en straf*, (*The safety utopy. Contemporary discomfort and desire around crime and punsihment*), The Hague: Boom Juridische Uitgevers.

Bovens, M. (2003) 'Zelfstandigheid tussen markt en meten', *Tijdschrift voor de Sociale Sector*, vol 57, pp 14-15.

Bowen, J. and Ford, R. (2002) 'Managing service organisations: does having a "thing" make a difference?', *Journal of Management*, vol 28, pp 447-69.

Bruner, J. (1975) 'From communication to language. A psychological perspective', *Cognition*, vol 3, pp 255-87.

Bruner, J. (1983) *Child's talk: Learning to use language*, New York, NY/London: Norton.

Bruner, J. (1990) *Acts of meaning*, Cambridge, MA: Harvard University Press.

Butler, I. and Drakeford, M. (2005) 'Trusting in social work', *British Journal of Social Work*, vol 35, pp 639-54.

Campbell, C. (1996) 'Detraditionalization, character, and the limits to agency', in P. Heelas, S. Lasch and P. Morris (eds) *Detraditionalization. Critical reflections on authority and identity*, Oxford: Blackwell, pp 149-69.

Campbell, R., Robinson, W., Neelands, J., Hewston, R. and Mazzoli, L. (2007) 'Personalised learning: ambiguities in theory and practice', *British Journal of Educational Studies*, vol 55, pp 135-54.

Camus, A. (2008; 1955) *The myth of Sysiphus*, Harmondworth: Penguin Books.

Chaiken, S. and Trope, Y. (1999) *Dual process theories in social psychology*, New York, NY: Guilford.

Chambers, R. (1997) *Whose reality counts? Putting the first last*, London: Intermediate Technology Development Group.

Chandler, M. (2000) 'Surviving time: the persistence of identity in this culture and that', *Culture & Psychology*, vol 6, pp 209-31.

Chandler, M. and Ball, L. (1990) 'Continuity and commitment: A developmental analysis of the identity formation process in suicidal and non-suicidal youth. In H. Bosma and S. Jackson (eds) *Coping and self-concept in adolescence*, New York: Springer-Verlag.

Chandler, M. and Proulx, T. (2008) 'Personal persistence and persistent peoples. Continuities in the lives of individual and whole cultural communities', in F. Sani (ed) *Self-continuity: Individual and collective perspectives*, New York, NY: Psychology Press, pp 213-36.

Chandler, M., Lalonde, C., Sokol, B. and Hallett, D. (2003) 'Personal persistence, identity development, and suicide. A study of native and non-native North American adolescents', *Monographs of the Society for Research in Child Development*, vol 68, pp 1-130.

Clarke, J. and Cochrane, A. (1998) 'The social construction of social problems', in E. Saraga (ed) *Embodying the social: Constructions of difference*, London: Routledge, pp 3-42.

Clarke, J. and Newman, J. (1997) *The managerial state*, London: Sage Publications.

Clarke, J., Gewirtz, S. and LcLaughlin, E. (2000) 'Reinventing the welfare state', in J. Clarke, S. Gewirtz and E. McLaughlin (eds) *New managerialism. New welfare?*, London: Sage Publications, pp 1-26.

Connolly, W. (1987) 'Modern authority and ambiguity', in J. Pennock and J. Chapman (eds) *Authority revisited*, Nomos XXIX, New York, NY: New York University Press, pp 9-27.

Cooper, A. and Webb, L. (1999) 'Out of the maze: permanency planning in a postmodern world', *Journal of Social Work Practice*, vol 13, pp 119-34.

Corveleyn, J. and Traversier, T. (1998) 'Inleiding. Het leven en het werk van Francoise Dolto', Introduction. Life and work of Francoise Dolto. in F. Dolto (ed) *Kinderen aan het woord. Psychoanalyse, kind en psychose*, (*Children speaking. Psychoanalysis, child and psychosis*), Nijmegen: SUN, pp 21-49.

Coté, J. and Levine, C. (2002) *Identity formation, agency, and culture. A social psychological synthesis*, Mahwah, NJ/London: Lawrence Erlbaum.

Custers, E., Boshuizen, H. and Schmidt, H. (1996) 'The influence of medical expertise, case typicality, and illness script component on case processing and disease probability estimates', *Memory and Cognition*, vol 24, pp 384-99.

Czarniawska, B. (1997) *Narrating the organization. Dramas of institutional identity*, Chicago, IL/London: University of Chicago Press.

Daly, G. (1999) 'Politics and the impossible. Beyond psychoanalysis and deconstruction', *Theory, Culture and Society*, vol 16, pp 75-98.

Davies, B. and Harré, R. (1990) 'Positioning: the discursive production of selves', *Journal of the Theory of Social Behaviour*, vol 20, pp 43-61.

Dean, M. (1999) *Governmentality. Power and rule in modern society*, London: Sage Publications.

de Jong, P. and Berg, I. (2001) 'Co-constructing cooperation with mandated clients', *Social Work*, vol 46, pp 361-75.

de Shazer, S. (1991) *Putting difference to work*, New York, NY: Norton.

de Winter, M. (1997) *Children as fellow citizens. Participation and commitment,* Oxford/New York, NY: Radcliffe.

Dijk, F. van and Bruins Slot, J. (2003) 'Meespelen met het management. Professionals in arbodiensten moeten zich organiseren', ('Playing together with the management. Professionals occupied at ARBO have to get organised'), *Medisch Contact*, vol 58, pp 1576-9.

Dolto, F. (1984) *L'image inconsciente du corps*, (*The unconscious image of the body*), Paris: Editions du Seuil.

Dolto, F. (1988a) *Tout est langage*, (*Everything is language*), Paris: Gallimard.

Dolto, F. (1988b) *Quand les parents se séparent*, (*When parents separate*), Paris: Editions du Seuil.

Dolto, F. (1994) *Les étapes majeures de l'enfance*, (*The major stages of infancy*), Paris: Gallimard.

Dolto, F. (1998) *Kinderen aan het woord. Psychoanalyse, kind en psychose*, (*Children speaking. Psychoanalysis, child and psychosis*), Nijmegen: SUN.

Donzelot, J. (1979) *The policing of families*, New York, NY: Pantheon.

Doolan, M. (1990) 'Youth justice reform in New-Zealand', *International Journal of Family Care*, vol 2, pp 77-90

Doornenbal, J. (1996) *Ouderschap als onderneming. Moeders en vaders over opvoeden in de jaren negentig*, (*Parenthood as undertaking. Mothers and fathers discuss bringing up children in the nineties*), Groningen: University of Groningen.

Drew, P. and Heritage, J. (eds) (1995) *Talk at work: Interaction in institutional settings*, Cambridge: Cambridge University Press.

DuBois-Reymond, M., Peters, E. and Ravesloot, J. (1990) 'Jongeren en ouders: van bevelshuishouding naar onderhandelingshuishouding', ('Youngsters and parents: from management by command to management by negotiation'), *Amsterdams Sociologisch Tijdschrift*, vol 17, pp 69-100.

Du Gay, P. (1999) 'In the name of "globalization": enterprising up nations, organizations and individuals', in P. Leisink (ed) *Globalization and labour relations*, Cheltenham: Edward Elgar, pp 78-93.

Du Gay, P. (2000) 'Entrepreneurial governance and public management : the anti-bureaucrats', in J. Clarke, S. Gewirtz and E. McLaughlin (eds) *New managerialism. New welfare?*, London: Sage Publications, pp 62-81.

Duintjer, O. (1977) *Rondom regels. Wijsgerige gedachten omtrent regel-geleid gedrag*, (*Around rules. Philosophical thoughts about rule-governed behaviour*), Amsterdam: Boom Meppel.

Duncan, G. and Brooks-Gunn, J. (2000) 'Family poverty, welfare, reform, and child development', *Child Development*, vol 71, no 1, 188-96.

Edwards, D. and Mercer, N. (1987) *Common knowledge. The development of understanding in the classroom*, London: Routledge.

Elbers, E. (1992) 'Children's contribution to their development as a theme in Vygotsky's work', *Comenius*, vol 12, pp 371-82.

Evans, T. and Harris, J. (2004) 'Street-level bureaucracy, social work and the (exaggerated) death of discretion, *British Journal of Social Work*, vol 34, pp 871-95.

Fairclough, N. (1991) *Discourse and social change*, Cambridge: Polity Press.

Fay, B. (1996) *Contemporary philosophy of social science*, Oxford: Blackwell.

Feinberg, J. (1980) 'The child's right to an open future', in W. Aiken and H. LaFollette (eds) *Whose child?*, Totowa, NJ: Rowman and Littlefield, pp 124-53.

Finch, J. and Mason, J. (1993) *Negotiating family responsibilities*, London: Routledge.

Flouri, E. (2005) *Fathering and child outcomes*, Chichester: Wiley.

Forrester, D., McCambridge, J., Waissbein, C. Emlyn-Jones, R. & Rollnick, S. (2008) 'Child risk and parental resistance: Can motivational interviewing improve the practice of child and family social workers in working with parental alcohol misuse? *British Journal of Social Work* vol 38, pp 1302-1319.

Foucault, M. (1979) *Discipline and punish. The birth of the prison*, New York, NY: Pantheon.

Foucault, M. (1980) *The history of sexuality. Volume I: An introduction*, New York, NY: Vintage.

Foucault, M. (1982) 'The dubject and the power', in H. Dreyfus and P. Rabinow (eds) *Foucault: Beyond structuralism and hermeneutics*, Brighton: Harvester, pp 208-26.

Foucault, M. (1985) *The use of pleasure: The history of sexuality. Volume 2*, New York, NY: Vintage.

Foucault, M. (1986) *The care of the self: The history of sexuality. Volume 3*, New York, NY: Pantheon.

Freeman, M. (1997) 'The best interests of the child? Is the best interests of the child in the best interest of children?', *International Journal of Law and the Family*, vol 11, pp 360-88.

Freidson, E. (1984) *Professional power: The study of the institutionalization of formal knowledge*, Chicago, IL: University of Chicago Press.

Froggett, L. (2002) *Love, hate and welfare. Psychosocial approaches to policy and practice*, Bristol: The Policy Press.

Frosh, S., Phoenix, A. and Pattman, R. (2003) 'Taking a stand: using psychoanalysis to explore the positioning of subjects in discourse', *British Journal of Social Psychology*, vol 42, pp 39-53.

Garfinkel, H. (1967) *Studies in ethnomethodology*, Englewood Cliffs, NJ: Prentice Hall.

Garner, P., Rennie, K. and Miner, J. (1996) 'Sharing attention to toys: adolescent mother-toddler dyads', *Early Development and Parenting*, vol 5, pp 101-10.

Gergen, K. and Gergen, M. (1983) 'Narratives of the self', in T. Sarbin and K. Schebe (eds) *Studies in social identity*, New York, NY: Praeger.

Gergen, K., Gergen, M. and Barrett, F. (2001) 'Toward a vocabulary of transformative dialogue', *International Journal of Public Administration*, vol 24, pp 697-707.

Gergen, K., Gergen, M. and Barrett, F. (2004) 'Dialogue: life and death of the organization', in D. Grant, C. Hardy, C. Oswick and L. Putnam (eds) *Handbook of organizational discourse*, Thousand Oaks, CA: Sage Publications, pp 39-60.

Giddens, A. (1984) *Central problems in social theory*, Cambridge: Polity Press.

Giddens, A. (1992) *The transformation of intimacy*, Cambridge: Polity Press.

Giddens, A. (1995) *Modernity and self-identity. Self and society in the late modern age*, Cambridge: Polity Press.

Gilligan, C. (1982) *In a different voice. Psychological theory and women's development*, Cambridge, MA: Harvard University Press.

Ginsburg, H. and Opper, S. (1969) *Piaget's theory of intellectual development*, Englewood Cliffs: Prentice Hall.

Glisson, C. (2002) 'The organizational context of children's mental health services', *Clinical Child and Family Psychology Review*, vol 5, pp 233-53.

Glisson, C. and James, L. (1992) 'The interorganizational coordination of services to children in state custody', in D. Bargall and H. Schmid (eds) *Organizational changes and development in human services organizations*, New York, NY: Haworth, pp 65-80.

Goffman, E. (1959) *The presentation of self in everyday life*, New York, NY: Doubleday.

Goffman, E. (1974) *Frame analysis: An essay on the organization of experience*, New York, NY: Harper.

Goffman, E. (1981) *Forms of Talk*, Philadelphia: University of Pennsylvania Press.

Goldstein, M., King, A. and West, M. (2003) 'Social interaction shapes babbling: testing parallels between birdsong and speech', *Proceedings of the National Academy of Sciences*, vol 100, pp 8030-5.

Griffith, W. (1999) 'The reflecting team as an alternative case teaching model. A narrative, conversational approach', *Management Learning*, vol 30, pp 343-62.

Grossen, M. (1996) 'Counseling and gatekeeping: definitions of the problem and situation in a first therapeutic interview', *Text*, vol 16, pp 161-98.

Grossen, M. and Apothéloz, D. (1998) 'Intelligence as a sensitive topic in clinical interviews prompted by learning difficulties', *Pragmatics*, vol 8, pp 239-54.

Grossen, M. and Salazar Orvig, A. (1998) 'Clinical interviews as verbal interactions: a multidisciplinary outlook', *Pragmatics*, vol 8, pp 149-54.

Gudykunst, W. and Kim, Y. (2003) *Communication with strangers*, Reading, MA: Addison-Wesley.

Gudykunst, W. and Nishida, T. (2001) 'Anxiety, uncertainty, and perceived effectiveness of communication across relationships and cultures', *International Journal of Intercultural Relations*, vol 25, pp 55-71.

Guidano, V. (1995) 'Constructivist psychotherapy: a theoretical framework', in A. Neimeyer and M. Mahoney (eds) *Constructivism in psychotherapy*, Washington, DA: American Psychological Association, pp 93-108.

Hall, C. and Slembrouck, S. (2009) 'Professional categorization, risk management and inter-agency communication in public inquiries into disastrous outcomes', *British Journal of Social Work*, vol 39, pp 280-98.

Hall, C., Slembrouck, S. and Sarangi, S. (2006) *Language practices in social work. Categorisation and accountability in child welfare*, London/New York, NY: Routledge.

Hall, E. (1976) *Beyond culture*, New York, NY: Doubleday.

Hallden, G. (1991) 'The child as project and the child as being: parents' ideas as frames of reference', *Children and Society*, vol 5, pp 334-46.

Harré, R. (1979) *Social being: A theory for social psychology*, Oxford: Basil Blackwell.

Harré, R. and Langenhove, L. van (1991) 'Varieties of positioning', *Journal for the Theory of Social Behaviour*, vol 21, pp 393-406.

Harris, J. (1998) 'Scientific management, bureau-professionalism, new managerialism: the Labour process of state social work', *British Journal of Social Work*, vol 28, pp 839-62.

Hart, S. (1991) 'From Property to Person Status. Historical perspective on Children's Rights'. *American Psychologist*, vol 46, pp 53-59.

Harvey, M., Mishler, G., Koenen, K. and Harney, P. (2000) 'In the aftermath of sexual abuse: making and remaking meaning in narratives of trauma and recovery', *Narrative Inquiry*, vol 10, pp 191-311.

Heelas, P., Lash, S. and Morris, P. (1996) *Detraditionalization. Critical reflections on authority and identity*, Oxford: Blackwell.

Held, V. (1993) *Feminist morality. Transforming culture, society, and politics*, Chicago, IL: University of Chicago Press.

Helwig, C. (1993) 'Commentary on Moshman', *Human Development*, vol 36, pp 41-4.

Hermans, H. (1996) 'Voicing the self. From information processing to dialogical interchange, *Psychological Bulletin*, vol 119, pp 31-50.

Hermans, H. (2001) 'The dialogical self: toward a theory of personal and cultural positioning', *Culture & Psychology*, vol 7, pp 243-81.

Hermans, H. (2004) 'Dialogical self: between exchange and power', in H. Hermans and G. Dimaggio (eds) *The dialogical self in psychotherapy*, Hove/New York, NY: Brunner-Routledge, pp 13-28.

Hermans, H. and Hermans-Jansen, E. (1995) *Self-narratives. The construction of meaning in psychotherapy*, New York, NY: Guilford.

Hermans, H. and Kempen, J. van (1993) *The dialogical self. Meaning as movement*, San Diego, CA: Academic Press.

Hjörne, E., Juhila, K. and Nijnatten, C. van (2010) 'Negotiating dilemmas in the practices of street-level welfare work', *International Journal of Social Welfare*, vol 20, pp 303-09.

Hochschild, A. (1989) *The second shift*, New York, NY: Avon.

Hochschild, A. (1997) *The time bind. When work becomes home and home becomes work*, New York, NY: Metropolitan.

Hofstede, G., Nijnatten, C. van and Suurmond, J. (2001) 'Communication strategies of family supervisors and clients in organizing participation', *European Journal of Social Work*, vol 4, pp 131-42.

Holland, S. (2004) *Child and family assessment in social work practice*, London: Sage Publications.

Holman, D. (2000) 'A dialogical approach to skill and skilled activity', *Human Relations*, vol 53, pp 957-80.

Holstein, J. and Gubrium, J. (2000) *The self we live by. Narrative identity in a postmodern world*, New York, NY/Oxford: Oxford University Press.

Honneth, A. (1995) *The struggle for recognition*, Cambridge: Polity Press.

Hoogenboezem, G. (2003) *Wonen in een verhaal. Dak- en thuisloosheid als sociaal proces*, (*Living in a story. Homelessness as a social process*), Utrecht: De Graaff.

Hoogsteder, M. (1995) *Learning through participation. The communication between young children and their caregivers in informal learning and tutoring situations*, Utrecht: University of Utrecht.

Hoogsteder, M., Nijnatten, C. van and Suurmond, J. (1998) 'Communication between family supervisors and mandated clients. An analysis of videotaped interactions', *International Journal of Child and Family Welfare*, vol 3, pp 54-71.

Jefferson, G. (2004) 'Glossary of transcript symbols with an introduction', in: G. H. Lerner (ed) *Conversation Analysis: Studies from the First Generation*. John Benjamins, Amsterdam, pp 13-31.

Jessop, B. (1997) 'The governance of complexity and the complexity of governance: preliminary remarks on some problems and limits of economic guidance', in A. Amin and J. Hausner (eds) *Beyond market and hierarchy. Interactive governance and social complexity*, Cheltenham: Edward Elgar, pp 95-128.

Johnson, D. and Johnson, R. (1996) 'Conflict resolution and peer mediation programs in elementary and secondary schools: a review of the research', *Review of Educational Research*, vol 66, pp 459-506.

Jordan, B. (1978) 'Comment on theory and practice in social work: a re-examination of a tenious relationship', *British Journal of Social Work*, vol 8, pp 23-5.

Jordan, B. (1987) 'Counselling, advocacy and negotiating', *British Journal of Social Work*, vol 17, pp 135-46.

Kaganas, F. and Diduck, A. (2004) 'Incomplete citizens: changing images of post-separation children', *The Modern Law Review*, vol 67, pp 959-81.

King, M. (1997) *A better world for children. Explorations in morality and authority*, London, Routledge.

Kliewer, W. and Sandler, I. (1992) 'Locus of control and self-esteem as moderators of stressor symptom relations in children and adolescents', *Journal of Abnormal Child Psychology*, vol 20, pp 393-413.

Kogos, J. and Snarey J. (1995) 'Parental divorce and the moral development of adolescents', *Journal of Divorce and Remarriage*, vol 23, pp 177-86.

Kohut, H. (1978) *Restoration of the self*, New York, NY: International Universities Press.

Komen, M. (1999) *Gevaarlijke kinderen, kinderen in gevaar. De justitiële kinderbescherming en de veranderende sociale positie van jongeren, 1960-1995*, (*Dangerous children. Children in Danger. Judicial child welfare and the changing social position of juveniles*), Utrecht: SWP.

Laan, P. van de (2000) 'Succes interventieproject is tevoren in te schatten: onderzoek en interventie bij jeugdcriminaliteit', ('The effect of intervention projects can be estimated before: research and intervention in juvenile criminality), *0/25*, vol 5, pp 21-5.

Labov, W. (1972) 'The transformation of experience in narrative syntax', in W. Labov (ed) *Language in the inner city: Studies in the Black English vernacular*, Philadelphia, PA: University of Pennsylvania Press, pp 354-96.

Lacan, J. (1949) 'The mirror stage as formative of the function of the I', in *Ecrits: A selection* (translation by A. Sheridan), New York, NY/London: Norton, pp 1-7.

Lacan, J. (1958) 'The signification of the phallus', in *Ecrits: A selection* (translation by A. Sheridan), New York, NY/London: Norton, pp 281-291.

Lacan, J. (1973) *The four fundamental concepts of psychoanalysis.* Harmondsworth: Penguin.

Laing, R. (1961) *The self and the others,* London: Tavistock.

Lalonde, C. and Chandler, M. (2004) 'Culture, selves, and time: theories of personal persistence in native and non-native youth', in C. Lightfoot, C. Lalonde and M. Chandler (eds) *Changing conceptions of psychological life,* Mahwah, NJ: Lawrence Erlbaum, pp 207-29.

Larson, R. (2006) 'Positive youth development, willful adolescents, and mentoring'. *Journal of Community Psychology,* vol 34, pp 677-689.

Leadbeater, C. (2003) *Personalisation through participation,* London: Demos.

Ledoux, M. (2004) *Waar zijn we toch mee bezig. Institutionele psychotherapie in weerstand en dialoog met de kwaliteitspsychiatrie, (Just what are we doing. Institutional psychotherapy in resistance and dialogue with quality psychiatry),* Kessel: Literarte.

Lefcourt, H. (1976) *Locus of control: Current trends in theory and research,* Oxford: Lawrence Erlbaum.

Le Grand, J. (2003) *Motivation, agency, and public policy: Of knights and knaves, pawns and queens,* Oxford: Oxford University Press.

Lemke, T. (2001) '"The birth if bio-politics": Michel Foucault's lecture at the Collège de France on neo-liberal governmentality', *Economy and Society,* vol 30, pp 190-207.

Lipsky, M. (1980) *Street-level bureaucrats. Dilemmas of the individual in public services,* New York, NY: Russell Sage Foundation.

Loeber, R., Slot, N. and Sergeant, J. (2001) 'Mythen ontmaskerd: verbanden tussen ontwikkeling, risicofactoren en interventies', Unmasking myths: relations between development, risk factors and interventions in R. Loeber, N. Slot, and J. Sergeant (eds) *Ernstige en gewelddadige jeugddelinquentie. Omvang, oorzaken en interventies, (Serious and violent juvenile delinquency),* Houten: Bohn, Stafleu and van Loghum, pp 345-55.

Lovlie, L. (1992) 'Postmodernism and subjectivity', in S. Kvale (ed) *Psychology and postmodernism,* pp 119-134.

Lozeau, D., Langley, A. and Denis, J. (2002) 'The corruption of managerial techniques by organisations', *Human Relations,* vol 55, pp 537-64.

Lyotard, J. (1984) *The postmodern condition; a report on knowledge,* Manchester: Manchester Unversity Press.

MacIntyre, A. (1981) *After virtue. A study in moral theory,* Notre Dame, IN: University of Notre Dame Press.

Mäkitalo, A. (2003) 'Accounting practices as situated knowing: dilemmas and dynamics in institutional categorization', *Discourse Studies,* vol 5, no 4, pp 495-516.

Mannoni, M. (1967) *L'enfant, 'sa maladie' et les autres, (The child, its 'illness' and the others),* Paris: Editions du Seuil.

Mannoni, M. (1976) *Un lieu pour vivre: Les enfants de Bonneuil, leurs parents et l'équipe des 'soignants', (A place to live: The children of Bonneuil, their parents and the team of 'carers'),* Paris: Editions du Seuil.

Mannoni, M. (1979) *La théorie comme fiction: Freud, Groddeck, Winnicott, Lacan, (The theory as fiction: Freud, Groddeck, Winnicott, Lacan),* Paris: Editions du Seuil.

Martin, J. (2006) 'Reinterpreting internalization and agency through G.H. Mead's perspectival realism, *Human Development*, vol 49, pp 65-86.

Martin, J., Sokol, B. and Elfers, T. (2008) 'Taking and coordinating perspectives: from prereflective interactivity, through reflective intersubjectivity, to metareflective sociality', *Human Development*, vol 51, pp 294-317.

McAuley, J., Duberley, J. and Cohen, L. (2000) 'The meaning professionals give to management … and strategy', *Human Relations*, vol 53, pp 87-116.

McMillen, J. (1999) 'Better for it: how people benefit from adversity', *Social Work*, vol 44, pp 455-69.

Miehls, D. and Moffatt, K. (2000) 'Constructing social work identity based on the reflexive self', *British Journal of Social Work*, vol 30, pp 339-48.

Miltenburg, R. and Singer, E. (1999) 'Culturally mediated learning and the development of self-regulation by survivors of child abuse: a Vygotskian approach to the support of survivors of child abuse', *Human Development*, vol 42, pp 1-17.

Mooij, A. (1975) *Taal en verlangen. Lacans theorie van de psychoanalyse*, (*Language and desire. Lacan's theory of psychoanalysis*), Amsterdam: Boom Meppel.

Mooij, A. (1985) 'De symbolische vader', The symbolic father in A. Ladan, P. Mettrop and W. Wolters (eds) *De betekenis van de vader. Psychoanalytische visies op het vaderschap*, (*The meaning of the father. Psychoanalytical visions of fatherhood*), Amsterdam: Boom Meppel, pp 43-52.

Mooij, A. (2010) *Intentionality, desire and responsibility. A study in psychopathology, psychoanalysis and law*, Leiden/Chicago, IL: Brill.

Mundy, P. and Gomes, A. (1997) 'A skills approach to early language development: lessons learned from research on developmental disabilities', in L. Adamson and M. Ronski (eds) *Communication and language acquisitions: Discoveries from atypical development*, Baltimore, MD: Paul Brookes, pp 107-39.

Muntigl, P. and Zabala, L. (2008) 'Expandable responses: how clients get prompted to say more during psychotherapy', *Research on Language and Social Interaction*, vol 41, pp 187-226.

Neimeyer, R. and Buchanan-Arvay, M. (2004) 'Performing the self. Therapeutic enactment and the narrative integration of traumatic loss', in H. Hermans and G. Dimaggio (eds) *The dialogical self in psychotherapy*, Hove/New York, NY: Brunner-Routledge, pp 173-89.

Newberger, E. (1980) 'The cognitive structure of parenthood: designing a descriptive measure', in R. Selman and R. Yando (eds) *Clinical-developmental psychology: New directions for child development 7: Clinical developmental research*, San Fransisco, CA: Jossey-Bass, pp 45-67.

Newman, J. (1998) 'Managerialism and social welfare', in G. Hughes and G. Lewis (eds) *Unsettling welfare: The reconstruction of social policy*, London: Routledge, pp 333-74.

Newman, J. (2002) 'Putting the "Policy" back into social policy', *Social Policy and Society*, vol 1, pp 347-54.

Nicolaï, N. (2003) 'Tegen het vergeten',Against forgetting in A. DeBruyne and W. Heuves (eds) *De ezel en de steen. Over psychoanalyse en herhaling*, (*The donkey and the stone. About psychoanalysis and repetition*),Amsterdam: Boom, pp 41-54.

Nijnatten, C. van (1988) 'Discourses in Dutch child welfare inquiries', *British Journal of Criminology*, vol 28, pp 494-512.

Nijnatten, C. van (1997) 'Tales of ordinary badness. Sexuality in Dutch child welfare discourse', *American Journal of Forensic Psychiatry*, vol 18, pp 51-67.

Nijnatten, C. van (2000) 'Authority relations in families and child welfare in the Netherlands and England: new styles of governance', *International Journal of Law, Policy and the Family*, vol 14, pp 107-30.

Nijnatten, C. van (2005) *Child and Family Social Work*, vol 10, pp 159-67.

Nijnatten, C. van (2006a) 'Finding the words. Social work from a developmental perspective', *Journal of Social Work Practice*, vol 20, pp 133-44.

Nijnatten, C. van (2006b) 'Meta communication in institutional talks', *Qualitative Social Work*, vol 5, pp 333-49.

Nijnatten, C. van (2010) 'Deadlocked dialogues in child welfare', *British Journal of Social Work*, vol 40, 826-40.

Nijnatten, C. van, Ackerveken, M. van den and Ewals, T. (2004) 'Managing assessment. Quality planning in assessment procedures of the Dutch Child Protection Board', *British Journal of Social Work*, 34, pp 531-40.

Nijnatten, C. van, Boesveldt, N., Schilperoord, A. and Mass, M. (2001) 'The construction of parental authority and cooperation in reports to the Dutch court'. *International Journal of the Sociology of Law*, vol 29, pp 237-252.

Nijnatten, C. van and Huizen, R. van (2004) 'Children of uxoricide: the construction of parenthood pathology in cases of family trauma', *Journal of Social Welfare and Family Law*, vol 26, pp 229-44.

Osborne, D. and Gaebler,T. (1992) *Re-inventing government. How the entrepreneurial spirit is transforming the public sector*, New York, NY: Penguin Books.

Parton, N. (1998) 'Risk, advanced liberalism and child welfare: the need to rediscover uncertainty and ambiguity', *British Journal of Social Work*, vol 28, pp 5-27.

Parton, N. (2000) 'Some thoughts on the relationship between theory and practice in and for social work', *British Journal of Social Work*, vol 30, pp 449-63.

Parton, N. and O'Byrne, P. (2000) *Constructive social work. Towards a new practice*, Houndmills/London: MacMillan.

Pawson, R. and Tilley, N. (1997) *Realistic evaluation*, London: Sage Publications.

Peräkylä, A. (2002) 'Agency and authority: extended responses to diagnostic statements in primary care encounters', *Research on Language and Social Interaction*, vol 35, pp 219-47.

Peterson, S. and Albers,A. (2001) 'Effects of poverty and maternal depression on early child development', *Child Development*, vol 72, pp 1794-813.

Piaget, J. (1968) *Six psychological studies*, New York, NY:Vintage Books.

Pollitt, C. (1990) *Managerialism and the public services*, Oxford: Basil Blackwell.

Polman, J. and Pea, R. (2001) 'Transformative communication as a cultural tool for guiding inquiry science', *Science Inquiry*, vol 85, pp 223-38.

Popper, K. (1959) *The logic of scientific discovery*, London: Hutchison.

Potter, J. (1996) *Representing reality. Discourse, rhetoric and social construction*, London: Sage Publications.

Prottas, J. (1979) *People-processing. The street-level bureaucrat in public service bureaucracies*, Lexington, MA: Lexington Books.

Prout, A. (2000) 'Children's participation: control and self-realisation in British late modernity', *Children and Society*, vol 14, pp 304-15.

Raddish, M., Horn, S. and Sharkey, P. (1999) 'Continuity of care: is it cost effective?', *The American Journal of Managed Care*, vol 5, pp 727-34.

Raes, K. (1996) 'De ethiek van het (forensisch) welzijnswerk en het veiligheidsbeleid. Tussen individuele rechtsaanspraken en punitieve ordeningspraktijken', ('The ethic of (forensic) welfare and security policy. Between individual judicial claims and punitive policies of order') *Panopticon*, vol 17, pp 570-91.

Redman, P. (2005) 'The narrative formation of identity revisited. Narrative construction, agency and the unconscious', *Narrative Inquiry*, vol 15, pp 25-44.

Riessman, K. (1993) *Narrative analysis*, Newbury Park, CA: Sage Publications.

Rogoff, B. (1990) *Apprenticeship in thinking: Cognitive development in social context*, New York, NY: Oxford University Press.

Rogoff, B., Paradise, R., Arauz, R., Correa-Chavez, M. and Angelillo, C. (2003) 'Firsthand learning through intent participation', *Annual Review of Psychology*, vol 54, pp 175-203.

Rommetveit, R. (1974) *On message structure. A framework for the study of language and communication*, London: Wiley.

Rommetveit, R. (1984) 'The role of language in the creation and transmission of social representations', in R. Farr and S. Moscovici (eds) *Social representations*, Cambridge: Cambridge University Press, pp 331-59.

Rommetveit, R. and Blakar, R. (1979) *Studies of language, thought and verbal communication*, London: Academic Press.

Rose, N. (1996a) 'The death of the social? Re-figuring the territory of government', *Economy and Society*, vol 25, pp 327-50.

Rose, N. (1996b) 'Authority and the genealogy of subjectivity', in P. Heelas, S. Lasch and P. Morris (eds) *Detraditionalization. Critical reflections on authority and identity*, Oxford: Blackwell, pp 294-327.

Rutter, M. (1987) 'Psychosocial resilience and protective mechanism', *American Journal of Orthopsychiatry*, vol 57, pp 316-33.

Saario, S. and Raitakari, S. (2010) 'Contractual audit and mental health rehabilitation: a study of formulating effectiveness in a Finnish supported housing unit', *International Journal of Social Welfare*, vol 20, pp 321-29.

Samovar, L., Porter, R. and McDaniel, E. (2006) *Communication between Cultures*, Oxford: Wadsworth Publishing Company.

Sampson, E. (1985) 'The decentralization of identity: toward a revised concept of personal and social order', *American Psychologist*, vol 40, pp 1203-11.

Sampson, E. (1988) 'The debate on individualism: indigenous psychologies of the individual and their role in personal and societal functioning', *American Psychologist*, vol 43, pp 15-22.

Schmittdiel, J., Selby, J., Grumbach, K. and Quesenberry, C. (1997) 'Choice of a personal physician and patient satisfaction in a health maintenance organization', *Journal of the American Medical Association*, vol 278, pp 1596-9.

Seikkula, J. (2002) 'Open dialogues with good and poor outcomes for psychotic crises: examples from families with violence', *Journal of Marital and Family Therapy*, vol 28, pp 263-74.

Sennett, R. (1998) *The corrosion of character. The personal consequences of work in the capitalism*, New York, NY: Norton.

Sennett, R. (2003) *Respect, in a world of inequality*, New York, NY: Norton.

Sevenhuijsen, S. (1998) *Citizenship and the ethic of care: Feminist considerations about justice, morality and politics*, London: Routledge.

Sheldon, B. (1978) 'Theory and practice in social work: a re-examination of a tenious relationship', *British Journal of Social Work*, vol 8, pp 1-22.

Sheldon, B. (1987) 'Implementing findings from social work effectiveness research', *British Journal of Social Work*, vol 17, pp 573-86.

Sheppard, M. (1995) 'Social work, social science and practice wisdom', *British Journal of Social Work*, vol 25, pp 265-93.

Sheppard, M. (1998) 'Practice validity, reflexivity and knowledge for social work', *British Journal of Social Work*, vol 28, pp 265-93.

Shotter, J. (1993) *Conversational realities: The construction of life through language*, London: Sage Publications.

Silva, E. and Smart, C. (1999) (eds) *The new family?*, London: Sage Publications.

Simpson, P., French, R. and Harvey, C. (2002) 'Leadership and negative capability', *Human Relations*, vol 55, pp 1209-26.

Singer, E., Doornenbal, J., and Okma, K. (2004) 'Why do children resist or obey their foster parents? A study of the inner logic of children's behaviour during disciplinary conflict', *Child Welfare*, vol 83, pp 581-610.

Skolnick, A. (1973) *The intimate environment: Exploring marriage and the family*, Boston, MA: Little Brown.

Slot, W., Theunissen, A., Esmeijer, F. and Duivenvoorden, Y. (2002) *909 Zorgen. Een onderzoek naar de doelmatigheid van de ondertoezichtstelling*, 909 Worries. A study of the efficiency of the family supervision order, Amsterdam: Vrije Universiteit.

Smart, C. (1997) 'Wishful thinking and harmful thinking? Sociological reflection on family policy', *Journal of Social Issues*, vol 26, pp 1-21.

Smart, C. and Neale, B. (1999) *Family fragments?*, Cambridge: Polity Press.

Smart, C., Neale, B. and Wade, A. (2001) *The changing experience of childhood. Families and divorce*, Cambridge: Polity Press.

Smeyers, P. (1992) 'Over macht en liefde in de opvoeding', ('About power and love in raising children') *Comenius*, vol 12, pp 301-25.

Smith, C. (2001) 'Trust and confidence: possibilities for social work in "high modernity"', *British Journal of Social Work*, vol 31, pp 287-305.

Smith, S. & Lipsky, M. (1993) *Nonprofits for Hire: The Welfare State in the Age of Contracting*, Cambridge, MA: Harvard University Press.

Sokol, B., Chandler, M. and Jones, C. (2004) 'From mechanical to autonomous agency: the relation between children's moral judgement and their developing theories of mind', *New Directions for Child and Adolescent Development*, vol 103, pp 19-36.

Stenson, K. (1993) 'Social work discourse and the social work interview', *Economy and Society*, vol 22, pp 42-76.

Stenson, K. and Watt, P. (1999) 'Governmentality and "the death of the social"?: a discourse analysis of local government texts in south-east England', *Urban Studies*, vol 36, pp 189-201.

Stiles, W. (1999) 'Signs and voices in psychotherapy', *Psychotherapy Research*, vol 9, pp 1-21.

Tappan, M. (1997) 'Language, culture, and moral development. A Vygotskian perspective', *Developmental Review*, vol 17, pp 78-100.

Sudermann, M. and Jaffe, P. (1997) 'Children and youth who witness violence, new directions in intervention and prevention', in D. Wolfe, R. Mc.Mahon and R. Peters (eds) *Child abuse. New directions in prevention and treatment across the lifespan*, London: Sage Publications, pp 55-78.

Sullivan, P. and McCarthy, J. (2004) 'Toward a dialogical perspective on agency', *Journal for the Theory of Social Behaviour*, vol 34, pp 291-309.

Tappan, M. (1997) 'Language, culture, and moral development. A Vygotskian perspective', *Developmental Review*, vol 17, pp 78-100.

Taylor, C. (1989) *Sources of the self*, Cambridge: Cambridge University Press.

Taylor, C. and White, S. (2000) *Practising reflexivity in health and welfare: Making knowledge*, Maidenhead: Open University Press.

Thompson, J. (1995) *The media and modernity: A social theory of the media*, Cambridge: Polity Press.

Thoms, P., Dose, J. and Scott, K. (2002) 'Relationships between accountability, job satisfaction, and trust', *Human Resource Development*, vol 13, pp 307-23.

Ting-Toomey, S. and Oetzel, J. (2002) 'Cross-cultural face concerns and conflict styles: current status and future directions', in W. Gudykunst and B. Mody (eds) *Handbook of international and intercultural communication*, Thousand Oaks, CA: Sage Publications, pp 143-63.

Trevarthen, C. (1979) 'Communications and cooperation in early infancy. A description of primary intersubjectivity', in M. Bullowa (ed) *Before speech: The beginning of human communication*, Cambridge: Cambridge University Press, pp 321-47.

Tronto, J. (1993) *Moral boundaries*, London: Routledge.

Turnell, A. (2010) *Building safety in child protection practice: Working from a strengths perspective*, London: Palgrave.

Valsiner, J. (2006) 'Dialogism: one or many?', Paper presented at 4th International Conference on the Dialogical Self, Braga, Portugal, 6 February.

Vandenbroeck, M. and Bouverne-de-Bie, M. (2006) 'Childeren's agency and educational norms. A tensed negotiation', *Childhood*, vol 13, pp 127-43.

VanDeVeer, D. (1986) *Paternalistic intervention. The moral bounds on benevolence*, Princeton, NJ: Princeton University Press.

Vanheule, S. and Verhaeghe, P. (2004) 'Powerlessness and impossibility in special education: a qualitative study on professional burnout from a Lacanian perspective', *Human Relations*, vol 57, pp 497-519.

Wel, F. van (1994) '"I count my parents among my best friends": youths' bonds with parents and friends in the Netherlands', *Journal of Marriage and the Family*, vol 56, pp 835-43.

Verbrugge, A. (2004) *Tijd van onbehagen. Filosofische essays over een cultuur op drift*, (*Times of discomfort. Philosophical essays about a culture adrift*), Nijmegen: SUN.

Verhaeghe, P. (1998) *Liefde in tijden van eenzaamheid. Drie verhandelingen over drift en verlangen*, (*Love in times of loneliness. Three essays about urge and desire*), Leuven/Amersfoort: Acco.

Verhellen, E. (1998) 'Children's rights: educations and academic responsibilities', in P. Jaffé (ed) *Challenging mentalities. Implementing the United Nations Convention on the Rights of the Child*, Ghent: Children's Rights Centre, University of Ghent, pp 97-123.

Verkujten, M. (2005) *The social psychology of ethnic identity*, Hove/New York, NY: Psychology Press.

Vygotsky, L. (1978) *Mind in society. The development of higher psychological processes*, Cambridge, MA: Harvard University Press.

Wastell, D., White, S., Broadhurst, K., Peckover, S. and Pithouse, A. (2010) Children's services in the iron cage of performance management: street-level bureaucracy and the spectre of Švejkism', *International Journal of Social Welfare*, vol 20, pp 310-20.

Webb, S. (2001) 'Some Considerations on the Validity of Evidence-based Practice in Social Work', *British Journal of Social Work*, vol 31, pp 57-79.

Wertsch, J. (1985) *Vygotsky and the social formation of mind*, Cambridge, MA: Harvard University Press.

Wertsch, J. (2008) 'From social interaction to higher psychological processes. A clarification and application of Vygotsky's theory', *Human Development*, vol 51, pp 66-79.

White, M. and Epston, D. (1990) *Narrative means to therapeutic ends*, New York, NY: Norton.

White, S. and Stancombe, J. (2003) *Clinical judgement in the health and welfare professions*, Maidenhead: Open University Press.

White, S., Hall, C. and Peckover, S. (2008) 'The descriptive tyranny of the Common Assessment Framework: technologies of categorization and professional practice in child welfare', *British Journal of Social Work*, vol 39, pp 1197-121. CHECK

Willemse, G., van Yperen, T. and Rispens, J. (2003) 'Reliability of the ICD-10 classification of adverse familial and environmental factors', *Journal of Child Psychology and Psychiatry*, vol 44, pp 202-13.

Winnicott, D. (1965) *The maturational process and the facilitating environment*, London: Hogarth Press.

Winnicott, D. (1985) *Playing and reality*, Harmondsworth: Pelican.

Wittgenstein, L. (1953) *Philosophical investigations*, Oxford: Blackwell.

Wittgenstein, L. (1969) *On certainty*, Oxford: Blackwell.

Wolff, P., Tesfai, B., Egasso, H. and Aradom, T. (1995) 'The orphans of Eritrea: a comparison study', *Journal of Child Psychology and Psychiatry*, vol 36, pp 633–44.

Wood, D. (1988) *How children think and learn. The social contexts of cognitive development*, Oxford: Blackwell.

Wyness, M. (1994) 'Keeping tabs on an uncivil society', *Sociology*, vol 28, pp 193–209.

Wyness, M. (1996) 'Policy, protectionism and the competent child', *Childhood. A Global Journal of Child Research*, vol 4, pp 431–47.

Young, I. (1990) *Justice and the politics of difference*, Princeton, NJ: Princeton University Press.

Zeithaml, V., Bitner, M. and Gremler, D. (2006) *Services marketing: Integrating customer focus on the firm*, Colombus, OH: McGraw-Hill.

Zelizer, V. (1994) *Pricing the priceless child. The changing value of children*, Princeton, NJ: Princeton University Press.

Žižek, S. (1991) *Looking awry: An introduction to Jacques Lacan through popular culture*, Cambridge, MA: MIT Press.

Žižek, S. (1992) *Enjoy your symptom!: Jacques Lacan in Hollywood and out*, New York, NY: Routledge.

Žižek, S. and Daly, G. (2004) *Conversations with Žižek*, Cambridge: Polity Press.

Appendix: Transcript conventions and abbreviations

?	sentence marked as question by grammar or intonation
(.)	short break (1-2 seconds)
[pause]	longer break (> 2 seconds)
°xxx°	softly spoken
<u>xxx</u>	with emphasis
(xxx)	probable speech
(?)	unintelligible, one or two words
(..?..)	unintelligible, longer fragment
[xxx]	text clarifying speech, inserted by transcribers e.g. [laughs]
[…]	part of conversation omitted
//	simultaneous speech
xxx/	(self)interruption

Source: Jefferson (2004)

Index

CHILDREN'S AGENCY, CHILDREN'S WELFARE

For Anneke